How Not to Start a Magazine

*Mistakes to avoid when starting your own
publication*

by
B. Ann Bell

Palfrey Media Publishing

Rough and Ready, CA

Table of Contents

Introduction   **1**

    The odds are against you   **2**
    Why do new magazines fail?   **2**

Chapter 1: Planning   **5**

    Plan for printing   **5**
    Plan for marketing   **12**
    Plan for postage   **13**
    Plan for office supplies   **15**

Chapter 2: Before you Begin   **16**

    Do this first: set up a website   **16**
    Websites: the hard stuff   **18**
    Find out if you have an audience   **22**
    Other pre-production dos and
    don'ts   **26**

Chapter 3: Your first issue   **27**

    Map out your magazine   **27**
    Finding a printer   **29**
    Finding writers   **30**
    Finding pictures   **35**
    To dummy or not to dummy?   **36**
    Advertising   **37**
    Pricing   **38**
    Layout   **38**
    Making it official   **41**

Chapter 4: After you've gone to press   44

Preparing for ad and subscription
sales   44
Accepting credit cards   49
I've got 5,000 copies in my
garage, now what?   51
Magazine distributors   52
Non-traditional outlets   54
Subscription brokers   56

Chapter 5: Marketing   58

You must market aggressively   58
Seeking advertisers   58
Seeking subscribers   60

Appendix A   66

Appendix B   71

Introduction

It came to you, perhaps, in a flash of divine inspiration—
a great idea for a new magazine. You've thought of a
unique new way of looking at a popular subject, or you
have some insider information you think people would
happily pay money to obtain. You're hoping your idea
will one day give you financial independence, or maybe
you'd just like an outlet for your creative energy. Either
way, you're sure there's a market for your magazine.
You're sure it will be a huge success.

All you have to have is a great concept, right?

Not exactly. You may indeed have a great concept, and it
may be targeting a niche market of people who are
hungry for information only you can provide. The
problem is, magazines do not sell themselves.

I made the mistake of believing that they do. My first
attempt at a magazine failed. But it wouldn't have, if I
had known then what I know today.

If you're serious about your venture, you've probably
already purchased some books on the subject. Many of
them will tell you that you must have an enormous
budget to succeed. Others will suggest expensive
marketing plans. They will tell you to do things that are
clearly outside your capacity to accomplish. Perhaps
you're feeling discouraged and overwhelmed. If so, let's
see if we can get your idea back on track. I can't
guarantee that your magazine will be everything you
dreamed it would be, but I can certainly help you to
increase your chances of success.

Who this book is for

This book is for the regular person, the average entrepreneur who does not have a gigantic throwaway income to devote to his or her new magazine project. This book is for the person embarking on a labor of love, the person with a big idea and a skinny budget. Despite what those other books tell you, it is actually possible to start a new magazine on a small budget and succeed. But you must be conservative.

The odds are against you

Sixty percent of new magazines fail before they are a year old. Worse, only five percent of new magazines will still be around by the time they reach their fifth year of publication. Those are ugly statistics. Yet when I started my magazine a couple of years ago, I believed I was exempt from the problems that caused other publications to fail. I had a great idea; the other 95 percent of the magazine-starting population probably did not. I soon discovered that having a great idea isn't enough.

Why do new magazines fail?

There are five regularly cited reasons for the failure of a new magazine:

1. **The magazine had an unrealistic budget**
   In my opinion, this is the big bad, the main killer of new magazines. New publishers often suffer from the erroneous belief that their magazine will sell itself. So they order excessively large print runs, they plan to produce their magazine far too frequently, they don't spend enough money on marketing, and they neglect to think about what their postage bill is going to be.
2. **The magazine has no audience or a narrow target audience**
   It's not enough to just ask your friends if they think you have a good idea. Most friends will say

"yes," even if inside they are thinking, "what the hell is she talking about?" It pays to do surveys of people who can be objective. Your parents do not count. Neither does your significant other.

3. **The magazine had poor quality editorial content**

Believe it or not, this really does happen. If you can't write and you have no editing skills, you need to find a partner. Your partner should be someone who is an accomplished (preferably published) writer. If you don't want a partner and you've never published anything yourself, consider taking some writing and editing classes. Ask your instructor what he/she thinks of your abilities. Be sure you can put together a quality product before you jump on the horse.

4. **The magazine didn't sell enough ads, or it appealed to advertisers who were already advertising somewhere else**

You'll only be excused from this burden for your first issue. After that, ad revenue needs to be pursued aggressively. Advertisers will rarely come to you, especially in the early stages of your magazine. If you must, hire someone to sell advertising for you. Also beware of market over-saturation—if there are already 27 magazines out there that appeal to your potential advertisers, you're going to have a hard time encouraging advertisers to leave the established venues in favor of your publication. You need to offer advertisers something they can't get in other magazines: a slightly different audience, for example, or a significantly better price. If you don't think you can overcome this hurdle, don't launch your magazine. Or, change your magazine's focus so this is no longer an obstacle to your success.

5. **The magazine wasn't able to get decent distribution**

It's very tough to beat this one. This can hurt new magazines in particular because they often can't afford to use distribution houses such as Magazania.com and Amazon.com (which typically only pay publishers about 10% of each subscription they sell). Traditional distributors pose a problem as well—they are often wary about new magazines, and if they do sign on they may buy only a few copies at a time. The key to getting enough distribution is to start early and be aggressive at pursuing opportunities.

Do not despair. Despite these obstacles, you can start a magazine, and you can succeed. The key is starting out very small and working your way up. The following chapters will tell you how.

Chapter 1: Planning

Plan for printing

If you're like me, your dream magazine is a beautiful thing to behold. It is full color, glossy, and at least 96 pages. It is loaded with expensive ads and beautiful pictures.

That is a lovely dream. Hang on to it for a while. Unless you've got several hundred thousand dollars to throw away, it will be a few years before that dream will come true.

Be pessimistic

This is sometimes the hardest thing to do. It is not in human nature to want to compromise, especially while engaged in a labor of love. You may think you aren't being true to your vision when you cut corners on things like color, length, and publication frequency. But try thinking of it this way instead—your labor of love could become a labor of nothing if you spend more than you can realistically afford.

A good rule of thumb is to plan your magazine based entirely on the money you have available to you right now. Assume you will sell nothing. Assume that no one will subscribe, and no one will buy advertising. I know it seems like a self-defeating way to budget for your labor of love, but it is not nearly as self-defeating as budgeting your magazine based on what you *think* you will be able to earn from it. The truth is, you can never really know how well your magazine will do. If you don't sell as many subscriptions as you would have liked, or you don't sell as many ads, a pessimistic budget will allow you to carry on publishing your magazine anyway. Alternately, if you've planned your budget based on money that you may or may not ever see, you run a much greater risk of failure. Finally, your pessimistic budget has the pessimistic benefit of protecting you from a lot of regrets if your magazine *does* fail. Believe me, nothing is quite so depressing as trying to pay down a $15,000 credit card bill for expenses related to a business you no longer own.

Cost cutting options you actually *don't* have

It is my belief that the cost of printing is the biggest single contributor to the failure of new magazines. The reason for this is very simple: volume. A sad truth about the printing industry is that nothing can be done cheaply in small quantities. If a new magazine could start out by printing, say, a premiere issue run of 250 copies, all magazines would survive. Unfortunately, that isn't the way it works.

When you purchase printing, a big chunk of what you're paying for is the cost of setting up the equipment. So 6,000 copies of your magazine is going to cost you only slightly more than 5,000 copies. My first print quote, for example, was for a four-color process magazine on 44 pages. I wanted to print 2,500 copies. I was quoted $5540.00; but for just $619 more I could have added another 1,000. Alternately, decreasing my order to 1,000 copies would have only knocked a few hundred dollars off my bill.

So simply put, you don't really have the option of saving money by printing fewer copies. You must start big. Which means you, the entrepreneur on a skinny budget, must find other ways to cut your printing costs.

Remember that the cost-cutting choices you make now don't have to be permanent. Your readers will have an easier time accepting your black and white magazine's transformation into a four-color magazine than your four-color magazine's demotion into a black and white magazine. You can always make improvements in the future when you have the budget for it. It's much more difficult to go backwards.

Following are some practical ideas on making your labor of love more affordable:

Go black and white

When I first considered launching my own magazine, I spoke to my college journalism professor about my idea. He advised me against a color publication on glossy paper. "Start small," he suggested. "You don't need to do color until you've generated enough interest in your magazine to pay for it."

I listened carefully to what he had to say and then I went ahead and did my magazine in color anyway. To my overly inflated sense of idealism, my magazine *needed* to be in color. It was a publication about art and culture; it had to have glossy color pictures because the subject matter demanded it.

Not true, of course. Few subject matters *demand* color, with the possible exception of food magazines, or perhaps magazines about paint. Even then, each page doesn't necessarily have to be in color. Most magazines have classified ad sections, or sections where advertisers can run inexpensive black and white ads. Even art magazines can have black and white sections; black and white photography looks beautiful in a glossy magazine. Don't think it is too much hassle to figure out how to produce a magazine that has a mixture of black and white and color. Your printer can explain how the layout will work. All you need to do is ask.

If you can, avoid color altogether in your first few issues and put it in your plan for future issues instead. If you absolutely feel your magazine must have color, have a color cover printed and do the inside pictures in black and white. Or do your magazine half color, half black and white. Just remember, the more color you add, the more expensive your printing bill will be.

Go twice yearly

A quarterly publication seems like a modest goal. Four times a year, how hard could that be? Depends. Do you have a staff of 12? Then you might be able to put out a quarterly magazine without completely demolishing your sense of freedom and alienating your friends, family, and spouse. If you're going it alone, though, there are a couple reasons why you shouldn't try to produce a quarterly magazine.

The first reason is time. If you are the number one and only employee of your magazine, you are going to wear a lot of hats. You're going to be editing. You're going to be writing. You're going to do the layout. You're going to sell ads, call distributors, design marketing campaigns, build and maintain your subscriber database, and you're going to stuff envelopes and go to the post office. And since you've got to come up with the money to pay for what you're doing, you're probably also going to be working at least part time at some job that actually generates income.

A twice-yearly publication is a much more realistic goal. You should be able to put together a twice-yearly magazine working a couple of nights a week, with plenty of time left over for pursuits of sanity (like walking the dog or going to the grocery store).

Another benefit to publishing twice yearly is that it gives your product a longer shelf life. The longer your magazine is on newsstand, the more people will see it there and the greater your chances will be of selling it. It also gives your marketing campaigns more time to work. Plus, your printing and postage bills will be just half of what they would be if you were producing a quarterly magazine. Though you probably won't be able to get away with charging as much for a twice-yearly subscription as you would for a quarterly, you will still earn more per subscription. Chances are, you won't be charging proportionally less money for a subscription (you may be able to get away with charging $9.95 for a twice-yearly subscription, while the same magazine produced quarterly bring in more like $14.95).

The only drawback to producing a twice-yearly publication is that you could have trouble finding distributors. Some distributors will only consider publications with a frequency of at least four times a year. This is something to keep in mind, especially if you are spending a lot of money on printing and you need to make sure you can sell copies quickly.

Go newsprint

Yuck! Newsprint?

Yes. When faced with a tight budget, sometimes it is best to start out by printing on uncoated paper. Have each printer you've obtained a quote from send you samples of the different kinds he or she has available. They're not all so bad. *E-Magazine*, for example, prints all its inside pages on uncoated stock, and it looks pretty good. Even newspaper-quality stock can be OK if your subject matter isn't terribly visual. Printing on uncoated paper can cut your costs significantly. If there's any way you can make it work, it's a good option to have.

Go shorter

This is a tricky cost-cutting method. If you are selling your magazine in the U.S., you've got the special challenge of penetrating an American psyche that believes bigger is always better. (If you need proof of this, go to a chain restaurant and order a plate of nachos.) As it turns out, people don't really care if your publication has fewer ads. Your 32-page magazine could have the exact same amount of editorial content as your similarly-priced 96-page competitor, but your potential readers will still think your competitor is the better bargain. Why? Because your competitor's magazine is bigger. It doesn't matter that the bigger part is 64 pages of ads that they probably aren't even interested in. The fact is, it's bigger, and to the American brain that means it is better.

There are a few ways you can combat this conundrum. First, have your magazine printed on heavier paper. This might cost a little more, but it doesn't cost as much as adding pages (which can be expensive in time as well as dollars). People who pick up your magazine aren't likely to count the pages, and they may think they're getting more for their money. Keep in mind, though, that one drawback to doing it this way is the cost of postage. Heavier magazines cost more to ship.

Second, charge less. I know, this seems painful, especially when you've just paid $2.20 for each one of the 2,500 magazines you have sitting in your garage. Unfortunately, the early stages of a magazine should not be about making money, they should be about attracting customers. If you aren't selling subscriptions at $14.95, lower your price to $11.95. If that doesn't work, lower it to $9.95. You'll still be bringing money in to help cover your expenses, but more importantly, you'll be attracting a larger number of people who may be willing to pay a higher subscription price when renewal time comes around.

Hell, just run it off at Kinkos

Obviously this is not a practical option for everybody. But if your subject matter is visually limited and your budget is really tight (you've received your estimate from the local printer and were aghast at the price of a 16-page black and white magazine on newsprint), it's something to consider. Hacking your labor of love down to a bi-folded newsletter may not be such a bad idea. If you have a really strong subject, if your content is specialized and if a lot of people are interested in it, your audience will probably be willing to overlook the fact that you've done your printing at the local copy mart.

A word about page count

When requesting estimates from printers, remember that magazines are usually printed in blocks of eight pages, which means your magazine can be 8 pages, 16 pages, 24 pages, 32 pages, 40 pages, 48 pages, etc. You can also produce a magazine with, for example, 44 pages—but if your printer's equipment prints in blocks of eight, it won't really save you any money (they'll trim off the extra paper, but you'll still have to pay for it). A web press is even more limiting—it prints in blocks of 16 pages, so you can only have a 16, 32, 48 page (etc.) magazine. Check with your printer to find out which format he or she uses, and plan your magazine accordingly.

Self cover vs. cover

Generally speaking, self-covered magazines are usually less expensive to print than covered magazines. "Self-covered' just means that you haven't chosen a different paper stock for the cover—it is printed on the same stock as the rest of the magazine. If you want a heavier stock for the cover, add a few hundred extra dollars on to the cost of your print run.

Consider an Internet-only publication

Internet-only magazines have less earning potential, but they also have far less overall expense. The main advantage is that you don't have to worry about printing and postage, which takes care of two of the three major expenses involved in publishing a magazine (the other one is marketing). However, unless your online magazine contains content that will a) help your subscribers make money or b) contains information that people desperately want but can't find anywhere else, you're going to have a hard time getting people to pay for a subscription. The Internet is already established as a "free" marketplace—chances are, if you ask your visitors to pay you they are going to simply say "hmph" and go somewhere else.

On the plus side, you can charge for advertising on your online magazine, but unless you're a very high traffic site (with 50,000 visitors each month or more), you probably won't get many takers and they probably won't pay as much to advertise with you. But there's a good chance that the revenue you'll generate from your website will, if you market your site correctly, pay for your expenses in a relatively short period of time.

Another advantage of an online magazine is that you can try out your idea on your readers and on yourself. You never know, six months into the project you may find that magazine publishing really isn't for you. You don't have the time, and you don't really have the motivation. Also, you may find that you just aren't able to attract readers to your editorial concept. Better to find out after one or two issues of an online journal than after one or two gigantic printing bills.

All things considered, if your magazine is primarily a labor of love and you aren't concerned about making a lot of money (now or in the future), you may want to go this route. It's definitely the lowest-risk way to produce a magazine. If you are afraid of the possibility of losing a lot of money (and even if you are extremely careful, a print magazine *always* poses a financial risk to its owner), consider doing an online magazine *before* you venture into print—or *instead* of venturing into print at all.

Plan for marketing

Here's another test many new businesses don't pass. They don't have a strong marketing budget.

Marketing is something a new magazine *must* budget for. With printing and postage, it is one of your top three expenses. But how can you decide how much you should spend on marketing? That depends partially on how much time you want to devote to your marketing plan (in general, if you don't have a lot of money to spend, you'll have to spend more time on less expensive but more time-consuming techniques such as search engine placement, passing out flyers, etc.). It also depends on how much money you have available.

You'll need to experiment in order to come up with a marketing plan that works for your particular editorial concept. A good rule of thumb is to start each campaign with a small test—for example, buy an ad banner on a high-profile website for one month. At the end of the month, compare the revenue from the ad to the amount of money you spent on it. Did you break even? Did you make money? Or did you come out of the campaign worse off than you were when you went into it? Base your decision to renew or expand the ad on how profitable it was. Never renew an ad that didn't at least pay for itself.

Finally, be honest with yourself about what you are willing to spend and how much financial loss you are willing to tolerate. If you've invested a great deal of money in a four-color print job and you aren't spending a lot of money on marketing, you could end up with a garage full of beautiful but unsold magazines. If you're willing to spend that kind of money on printing, you need to be willing to spend a proportional amount on marketing. If you can't afford to do both, don't do either. Or, at the very least, trade the four-color print job for black and white, and put the leftover money into your marketing campaign. As antithetical as it may seem, the marketing campaign should always get priority over the quality of the publication. It's much better to sell all of your black and white magazines than to sell just a few of your color magazines.

Plan for postage

For some reason, this is one of those things people don't think about. But postage kills new magazines just as surely as poorly planned printing does.

My 48-page magazine cost $1.29 to mail. It was a quarterly magazine, so that added up to $5.19 of the $14.95 I was getting for each subscription—nearly 35% of my earnings. But, you may be thinking, don't periodicals get a special rate from the U.S. Postal Service? Yes. Primedia and Time Warner get a special rate from the U.S. Postal Service, but independent publishers like you and me can't count on the same kickbacks. Getting the special periodical rate is difficult. The post office doesn't really want you to have it, so they haven't gone to any great lengths to make it easy for you to get.

First of all, you can't qualify for the periodicals rate if you only publish twice-yearly; you must be at least quarterly. You also have to have less than 75% advertising in half of each year's issues (usually no problem for startup magazines), and (here's the clincher), you have to have more than 50% paid circulation.

Unfortunately, to the U.S. Post Office "paid' circulation means that you must sell half of whatever you had printed. So even if 4,000 of your 5,000 copies remain in your garage after the publication cycle has ended and you sold the other 1,000, you'll still fail the post office's test for 50% paid circulation. Those extra 4,000 copies count as freebies, even if they never get any further than your garage. Unless you somehow managed to find a printer who can print small quantities cost-effectively, the chances are pretty good that it will be a long time before you can qualify for the periodicals rate. Hence, it's very dangerous to plan your budget around the possibility that you might get a special postage rate. Plan instead on paying the same rate as the rest of us suckers.

This means knowing ahead of time how much your magazine will weigh. When you're going after print estimates, be sure to ask each printer to send samples of magazines they've printed that are of the same length and the same stock as you are planning to use. Then put the sample in an envelope and weigh it. Budget your postage costs based on that.

Finally, buy a postage scale. You'll also need a postage metering machine, or you'll need to sign up for Stamps.com (www.stamps.com). By doing this, you'll save yourself a gigantic headache and several thousand dollars in gasoline from driving back and forth to the post office every day. Plus, you won't have the added bad karma of having everyone at the post office hate you (the first time you show up at the post office with a box of 100 magazines, you'll know exactly what I mean).

The light at the end of the tunnel

It's not all doom and gloom as far as your postage bill is concerned. The U.S. Post Office has recently announced a new set of discounts for independent magazines— though the average novice publisher may have a difficult time understanding how they work. For details, visit the Independent Press Association at www.indypress.org.

Plan for office supplies

This is another thing people forget to budget for. You will need envelopes. Lots of them. You'll need envelopes printed with your logo and address—both return addressed envelopes (number 10) and envelopes people can use to send payments to you (number 9, so they'll fit snugly inside your number 10). You'll also need a laser printer (ink jet looks very unprofessional), large envelopes, business cards, address labels, and folders for your media kits. For a complete list of start-up musts, visit the appendix at the end of this book.

Chapter 2: Before you Begin

Do this first: set up a website

Here is the cardinal rule for launching a new magazine on a tight budget: you must have a website. This will be your number one marketing tool and the number one way you will attract new subscribers. A website can be built cheaply and it can be promoted cheaply. You can use it to accept credit card payments, you can use it to establish a market for your product, and you can use it to glean whether or not a market even exists.

But I don't know anything about websites!

That's OK. You'll learn. HTML is not difficult. In fact, it's so easy a trained monkey could do it. If you don't have a trained monkey, buy "HTML for Dummies" or some similar product. Or, just go to one of the many online tutorials that will show you how to put together a website. The URLs for some of the better ones are listed in the appendix at the end of this book.

The basics of your website

So you've just read the last paragraph and you've signed up for your free Geocities website. You're all set to build your homepage.

Now, dump your free Geocities website. I know you have a skinny budget, but you're not allowed to be that cheap. Nothing says "amateur" quite so explicitly as a Geocities website. And nothing annoys your visitors and potential customers quite as much as all those flishy-flashy banner ads and pop-up windows.

You need a real website. This means registering a domain name and paying for a hosting account. Relax, it's not that expensive. Domains can be registered for less than $10 a year now; decent hosting accounts are available for about $10 a month. Compared to what you'll spend on marketing your magazine elsewhere, this is a bargain.

Your website should contain a couple of basic elements:

1. **An introduction to your magazine and your editorial concept**
   On your homepage, let your potential customers know exactly what you're all about. Let them know why you started the magazine and what kind of material you plan to print in it.

2. **A place where people can subscribe**
   In the early stages, just offer a sign-up form that people can use to "reserve" a subscription. This will also help you gauge interest in your idea. If you don't know how to build a contact form, I've included some simple code in the appendix at the end of this book (*Note: You will need an ASP capable website to use it. If you're not sure if you have an ASP capable website, ask your hosting provider*).

3. **A place where people can read the first paragraphs of each story in your current issue**
   Obviously, you won't be able to do this until you actually have current issues, but in the future this feature will be useful to you for a number of reasons. First, it will encourage people to buy a copy, especially if they've stumbled upon your "current issue" page while searching the Internet for a subject that your current issue just happens to cover. Second, it will eventually earn you greater search engine exposure. The more current issue summaries you have online, the more keywords you'll have for the search engines to archive. This will help you build traffic.

4. **Advertising information**
   Potential advertisers need to know how to contact you. You should post your ad rates as soon as you've figured out what they're going to be (see "Pricing your Ads" in Chapter 4), and you should include a sign-up form (just like your subscription reservation form) where potential advertisers can let you know what kind of ad they are interested in.

5. **Writer's guidelines**
   A lot of magazine websites don't include these, but unless you're planning on writing the whole thing yourself (a bigger task than you might imagine), having your guidelines online will help you attract freelancers. It will also, believe it or not, help you sell magazines. You want your potential writers to understand your magazine and the kinds of stories you buy, and an added plus is that every potential freelancer is also a potential paying customer.

The hard stuff

You must now learn the ins and outs of marketing on the Internet. Many people believe that "if you build it, they will come." Not true. Your website must be listed on every major search engine. There must be a link to it on as many portal sites as you can find. It must be optimized so that search engines not only know about it, they put it at the top of their keyword searches. All of these things are enormously important to the success of your online marketing campaign.

Search engines

Your first task is to become an expert at search engine optimization. One of the best places online to do this is www.selfpromotion.com. This website has at least a dozen extremely useful tools that will help you understand how to achieve a strong listing for your website, and it also has a service that will submit your site to multiple search engines (so you won't have to go to each and every one to enter the same information). Selfpromotion.com survives on donations, so if you use this service please send the site's owner a few bucks.

Portal sites and links directories

Find out what the most popular websites are that appeal to your potential audience. For example, if your magazine is aimed at cat owners, go to www.yahoo.com and do a search for "cats." Then click on the category listings Yahoo! returns (in this case, *Mammals > Cats*). Yahoo! will tell you what its most popular listings are in that category. Many of these sites will have links directories; most of them will allow you to submit your link for free. Be sure to do this on each of the popular websites, and any of the less popular ones you think might also be high traffic sites (some sites will tell you how much traffic they get, others may have an active message board, a professional look and feel, or some other indication that they attract a significant number of visitors).

After you've submitted your site to the popular websites, go back to Yahoo! and do a search for "cat links." Submit your site to as many of these hits as you can. Don't be lazy on this task; the more sites you submit to, the more traffic you will generate, and the more potential customers you will attract.

Banner ads

These can be useful, but be wary. Some of them do not pay for themselves. You should first look into banner advertising with those "most popular" websites you found on your Yahoo! search. Those sites are likely to give you the best return, though they are also likely to be a bit more expensive. Be careful, too, about how they plan to charge you. I generally like to stay away from websites that bill "per impression," which basically means that every time a user loads a page with your banner on it, you will get charged. It doesn't matter if that user never actually scrolled down to see your

banner, or if he or she ignored it altogether. You'll get
charged regardless. It's much better to go for sites that
charge per click (which means a user actually has to pay
attention to your banner before you have to pay
anything), or sites that charge a flat monthly rate.

Pay per click search engines

Pay per click search engines are, in my opinion, the
future of Internet advertising. The reason is because it is
extremely difficult to get high search engine placement
the traditional way, even if you do everything by the
book. You just have way too much competition.

Pay per click is not terribly expensive, despite how it may
sound. My pay per click account with Overture
(www.overture.com) (the only place, as far as I'm
concerned, where you should bother to go for pay per
click advertising) costs just over $25 a month, and it
generates more than enough sales to pay for itself.

Pay per click works like this: you choose the search terms
you think will be most likely to generate traffic for your
site, and you "bid" on them. When a user visits one of the
pay per click service's partner search engines and
searches for a term you bid on, your listing will appear at
or near the top of the search results (as a "sponsored
link"), depending on how much you bid for that listing.
The highest bid receives the top position.

Some of the smaller pay per click search engines let you
bid cheaply (often starting at as little as 01¢), but that
doesn't do you much good if there isn't anyone using
those engines. Overture search results appear on nearly
every major search engine, including Yahoo!, which is
the single most important place to be listed.

Here's an example of how pay per click works. Let's say
your magazine is aimed at model airplane collectors, so
you decide you want to bid on the search term "model
airplane." You log into your Overture account, you click
on the Search Term Suggestions tool, and you search for

"model airplane." The tool tells you that last month, more than 45,000 people searched for the words "model airplane" on Overture's partner websites. It also tells you that the highest bid to date is 51¢, which means you'll have to bid at least 52¢ if you want the top spot. But, maybe you can do better. A more refined search reveals that substantially fewer people searched for "model airplane magazine" (just 660), but the bidding on that search term is only up to 11¢. Which one should you bid on?

"Model airplane magazine" is much more targeted than "model airplane." Even though you won't pay nearly as much for it, it could generate better results than the more expensive listing. "Model airplane magazine" is a *qualified* lead, which means that each of the 660 people who search for the term are going to be far more likely to be interested in your product than each of the 45,000 people who searched for "model airplane." You want to attract people who are searching specifically for model airplane magazines, because they are going to be more likely to buy your product than people who are just looking for general information about model airplanes. You'll get fewer clicks with that search term, but they will be much more cost effective. That doesn't necessarily mean you shouldn't bid on both listings, but you will probably sell more subscriptions to the second group than to the first.

One word of caution: when signing up for an Overture.com account, it pays to know what you are getting yourself into. Don't listen to Overture when they suggest that you always include the search term you bid on in your listing headline, "because it will help you achieve a higher click-through rate." Yes, following those instructions will get you a higher click-through rate, but that benefits Overture more than it benefits you. You don't necessarily want a higher click through rate; you want a higher sell-through rate. That means your listing needs to let people know exactly what you are selling before they click. If the searcher isn't interested in model airplane magazines, you don't want to pay 52¢ for that person to click on your headline. You want that person to know you're selling a model airplane magazine—so make sure you're very clear about that in the listing, regardless of which search term you've chosen to bid on.

Also, beware of making it look like you've got any free information on your site. A lot of people search the web because they want to find some specific piece of information, not because they are looking to spend any money. For instance, if your magazine is a how-to publication focusing on, say, making money as a freelance writer, don't make your pay per click listing look as if your site has free articles or information on the subject, or you've just paid a pocketful of change in order for your visitor to find out that you don't have what he or she is looking for. Examples of how to avoid this mistake:

> **Bad:**
> Freelance Writing Today: Features articles and advice on how to make money as a freelance writer.

> **Good:**
> Freelance Writing Today: Subscribe to "Freelance Writing Today," the only magazine guaranteed to help you make money as a freelance writer.

Now find out if you have an audience

Now that you have your website, you also have a tool you can use to test your editorial concept. I have already mentioned this once, but it is worth repeating: make sure you have an audience before you spend any money on anything else. The simple fact that you think you have a good idea may not be enough to support your magazine. Someone somewhere probably thought there was a market for *Clog Dancing Quarterly*, too, but you won't find that title at any Barnes & Noble.

This doesn't mean asking your friends and family, because they will probably not be completely honest with you. You need to ask complete strangers, people who won't care about hurting your feelings.

I, too, balked at the idea of spending money on preliminary surveys. It does seem very much like stuffing dollar bills into envelopes and tossing them from a freeway overpass. But the return you will get on your investment could save you from a lot of future pain. And you don't have to spend a lot of money, either.

Rule number one: stay away from mailing list rentals

Mailing list rentals are stupidly expensive. Most list rental houses will get you a mailing list for about $250 per 1,000 names. Not so bad if you could just buy 1,000 names—but the catch is that there will usually be a 5,000-name minimum. So going with a list rental house will cost you a minimum of $1,250—and that doesn't include what you'll spend on the design of your mailer, printing, envelopes, and postage. Not such a good deal after all.

So what can you do? Email list rentals are a much more economical alternative. But wait, you gasp, isn't that spam? Can be, if you don't do it carefully. The key words here are "double opt-in." Companies that deal in double opt-in lists have asked all their participants to sign up for their mailing lists, and they have then verified that the person who signed up each email address is actually the person who owns that address. Double opt-in lists always put an "unsubscribe" link at the bottom of each mailing, but more to the point, the "unsubscribe" link actually does something (many unsolicited emails include "unsubscribe" links that go nowhere).

You also need to be sure you are going to a reputable firm. Some email list companies might not be so honest about how they get their names and whether or not their list is truly a double opt-in. To be sure, check their list of clients—if they are serving names you recognize, like American Airlines or Ford, they are probably reputable. If they are serving a company that sells Viagra or ink jet refills, I'd be a lot less likely to trust them.

If you decide to go with an email list, you'll need to send recipients to your website to fill out your survey. It helps if you can offer some kind of reward for participation, such as a chance to win a prize. It doesn't have to be a big prize, just something that people would gladly trade five minutes of their time for a chance to own. For your model airplanes magazine, for example, this might be a $35 die-cast model F-16, or some similarly priced item. Beware of offering free magazine subscriptions as prizes; if your magazine fails, you'll have to come up with some other kind of compensation for the remainder of your winner's subscription, and this is one more headache you don't need.

What to put on the survey

Keep your survey short (you don't want to overwhelm people). Ask maybe six to eight questions. Focus the first few questions on your visitor's personal tastes, for example:

1. Do you collect model airplanes?
2. Do you prefer die-cast or plastic models?
3. Do you build models, or do you buy ready-made models?

Focus the next couple of questions on the magazine concept itself:

4. What model airplane topics do you enjoy reading about?
5. What model airplane magazines do you currently subscribe to?
6. Would you purchase or subscribe to a magazine about die-cast model airplanes?

Finally, ask one or two questions that require some typing on the part of the user (don't ask too many of these, as people might be scared off):

7.   What would you most like to read about in a model airplane magazine?
8.   What kind of information is missing from the model airplane magazines you currently subscribe to?

The most important question on the survey, obviously, is number six. If the overwhelming answer to this question is "no," you may want to rethink your idea. That doesn't mean you shouldn't go ahead and do your magazine, it just means you should pay more attention to the answers given to questions number seven and eight. If your visitors don't want the die-cast model airplane magazine, what kind of magazine do they want? Perhaps you'll need to tweak your idea a bit, or revamp it altogether.

Don't give too much away

One fear many new publishers have is that a bigger, better-funded publisher will come along and steal their idea. If this is you, be sure to cover your tracks. Keep your online survey limited and temporary. Keep the survey on your website for as long as it takes to get results, then delete it. Don't just remove all links to it (search engines might still be able to find it), delete it from the website entirely.

At the same time, don't be too paranoid. The chances of another publisher stealing your idea are pretty slim, even if they know about you *and* they think your idea is the best thing since Oprah. If a publisher is actively thinking about starting a new magazine, he or she probably already has plans and isn't going to completely change direction in order to steal your concept. If a publisher is not actively thinking about starting a new magazine, the chances are pretty slim that he or she even has the budget to steal your idea. It's OK to guard your idea, but not if it means you're guarding it from potential subscribers as well as potential thieves.

Other pre-production dos and don'ts

Join the IPA

It's a very good idea to join some kind of professional organization, such as The Independent Press Association (www.indypress.org). Their email list alone is enough to pay for the cost of membership. Joining the IPA means you'll always have access to advice from within the independent publishing industry. You can network with other publishers (many of whom have years of experience available to share with you), and you can call the IPA directly with any questions or concerns you have about your business. They publish a number of reports on key points of the publishing business, such as attracting advertisers, getting new subscribers, etc. They also have their own in-house distribution service (which is only available to qualified publishers, but if you qualify it's definitely worth its weight in membership dues).

Chapter 3: Your first issue

Plan your magazine

The format of most magazines follows a very specific three-part formula: features, columns, and departments. Decide on all three before you begin publishing your magazine.

Readers like consistency, so having this three-part structure is important. Your readers will quickly develop favorite sections—parts of your magazine they'll read first, save for last, or look for if they only have a few minutes to kill. It's no good establishing departments and columns and then yanking them away at random. Once you have your magazine's basic structure, you'll need to stick with it for a while.

Columns

A column is usually written by the same person every month. Columns can include your editorial (you will have one, won't you?), advice from an expert, comments from an industry insider, or whatever you think might appeal to your audience. Columns are also useful because you don't need to come up with a new idea for them every month (the column's author will do that for you), and you don't need to spend a lot of time chasing down contributors. Once the column is established, you can keep it around indefinitely.

Work hard at locating trustworthy people for your columns. You don't want to experience the feeling of panic that comes with trying to fill an empty page in your magazine 24 hours before press day because your regular columnist flaked on her deadline. If a columnist shows any sign of unreliability (she asks you for a deadline extension, she doesn't answer your emails or return your phone calls), drop her *before* you ever publish one of her columns. You don't want your readers to get used to seeing her column and then wonder why it disappeared four issues later. If a writer is unreliable, you'll usually be able to tell by the way she handles her first assignment.

Departments

Like a column, a department is something that appears regularly in your magazine. Unlike a column, it can be written by a different contributor every month, or it may not have a byline at all (letters to the editor fall into this category; so do shopping guides, classified ads, or short pieces that focus on the same subject each month). Departments are the corner stone of your publication, and they are a big part of what gives it its unique flavor.

To come up with ideas for your magazine's regular departments, look at the departments in competing magazines. Think about how your magazine might do better. Come up with a new slant on one of their themes, or try to find something completely unique. Be careful not to duplicate anything they're doing, or your readers might think you don't have any unique ideas.

Features

Feature articles are the meat of your magazine. These are usually longer pieces (1,000 to 3,000 words), and they are unique to every issue. Feature stories are often based on ideas that freelancers submit, or they may be generated by the editorial staff (or you, provided you don't have an editorial staff). The only rule features need to follow is that they should be consistent with your editorial mission, that is, your "Make Money as a Freelancer" magazine shouldn't really run any features that discuss writing for charity—unless you can somehow claim that your charity work will lead to more paying jobs.

Find a printer

One of the first things you'll have to do is locate a printer. Printing prices vary wildly—and for no really apparent reason—so you will have to shop around. My first couple of quotes came in at around $7,000 for 2,500 four-color 44-page magazines. I refused to accept this totally outlandish price, and I eventually found a printer who would do it for about $5,400—but I had to contact several dozen different shops before I found the right one. The shop I finally settled on was Canadian, and they saved me about $1,000 over the next cheapest estimate I'd seen. Then, after my second issue went to press, another printer contacted me with an offer to print twice as many copies of my third issue for just over $5,000. So don't assume that all printers are priced competitively. Often they are not.

Get samples

If a printer's price sounds too good to be true, it probably is. Be sure to ask for samples from any printer you are seriously considering. Make sure that the quality of their work is what you envision for your magazine. Familiarize yourself with their paper stock, the way the colors look, and the way the magazine has been trimmed (are the edges smooth, are the margins comfortable or has the magazine been trimmed too close?). Be very selective. If you see anything you don't like, ask the printer to explain it. If you aren't happy with the quality, don't use the printer.

Ask about web printing

If you don't know what a web-press is, a printer who doesn't offer web printing isn't going to volunteer that information. Web printing is cheaper, although you have to print a relatively high volume to take advantage of it. You won't spend any less on it than you would with a sheet-fed solution, but you'll get more for your money. Unless you are going to start by printing as little as possible (which is not really very cost-effective), it's worth asking about web printing.

Finding writers

Don't try to write the whole magazine yourself. For one thing, you'll be suicidal before you get to page nine. For another thing, (contrary to what you may think), it just doesn't look very impressive to the average reader. If your name is on every byline, people aren't going to take your magazine very seriously. Unless you are a recognized expert in your field, most potential readers will think you're some kind of egomaniac if you're the only contributor to your own magazine. Also, it just doesn't look very professional. If you can't find contributing writers, people aren't going to take you very seriously. You'll seem unprofessional, even "tainted" by the lack of interest writers apparently have in your publication.

Don't despair, though. Freelancers are easy to find. Writers, especially new writers, are eager to get clips. A lot of them will write for free, but that doesn't mean you should ask them to write for free. For one thing, asking a writer to work for free is unethical. It's a lot like asking someone to wash your car for free. Writers may love to write (perhaps more so than the neighbor kid loves to wash your car), but writing is still work. It still takes time, and writers need to pay the bills too. But there are also other reasons why you should pay your freelancers. If you don't offer any financial compensation, you're really limiting your ability to market yourself as a legitimate market for freelancers.

That doesn't mean you have to pay a lot. If your magazine is losing money (and it most likely will, especially for the first couple of years), there's no reason why you should have to pay several hundred dollars for each article you use. Doing so will kill your magazine just as fast as a badly budgeted print run or an unsuccessful marketing campaign.

Many freelancers will not understand this. To them, all magazines (large and small) are money-generating machines. All publishers are driving around in Lexus SUVs that they are only able to afford because they have grossly underpaid their writers. You must learn not to take snubs from offended writers personally. Be sure your payment plan is well publicized, so that writers who are "too good for you" will avoid submitting their ideas to you in the first place.

How much should I pay?

I believe that a new magazine is reasonable in offering $25 for features and $10 for shorter pieces (with a couple of contributor copies thrown in for good measure). If your pay scale is that low, though, be sure to buy only first North American Serial Rights. That means the writer will be free to submit his article elsewhere after it has appeared in your magazine. Buying all rights from a writer you're only paying $25 to is just as unethical as not paying him at all. When you've got a bigger budget, you can start purchasing more rights. But don't ask someone to put hours into writing an article for you, and then take away his right to get additional revenue from all that work at a later time.

Offering small compensation also opens up a lot of different channels for publicizing yourself as a freelance market. A lot of freelance websites and market books (such as "Writer's Market") will only list paying markets. Asking writers to work for free will exclude you from those resources, and those resources can be a source of revenue as well as a source of talent.

Write your guidelines

Before submitting yourself to the freelance websites and market books, you'll need to establish your writer's guidelines. You should put these on your website, and you should also have printed copies available for writers who choose to contact you by surface mail.

Writer's guidelines should contain the following information:

1. **Your editorial/mission statement**
   This is one or two sentences that will tell a writer what your magazine's emphasis is.

2. **Articles published**
   Put your list of subjects here. For example, your model airplane magazine might be looking for articles on antique models, current trends in models, reviews of new products, profiles of modelers, book reviews, etc.

3. **Audience**
   Give potential freelancers as much information about your audience as you can. This can be difficult for a new magazine to do, because you haven't yet conducted any reader surveys that will tell you things like age, income level, education, etc. But you can get at least a general idea about your readership by looking at demographics for magazines with a similar focus (these demographics are usually listed in the "advertising" section of a magazine's web site).

4. **Submissions**
   Here is where you let writers know how they should contact you. To make it easy on yourself, ask for query letters (article proposals). Don't ask for complete manuscripts. You'll get inundated with stuff you don't want to read, and don't have the time to read anyway.

5. **Assignments**
   Tell writers how you assign articles. Usually this just means explaining that they'll have to sign a contract (more about contracts later in this chapter).

6. **Length**
   Provide a general guideline for the average number of words in a feature article and/or a column.

7. **Photographs**
   Let writers know whether or not you're looking for photos and/or art, and how such work should be submitted (ie., slides, prints, email, etc.).

8. **Departments**
   List your magazine's departments and describe what goes in each of them.
9. **Payment**
   This is very important. Don't be afraid you'll scare a writer off by saying upfront how much (or how little) you pay. If a writer doesn't want to write for $25, he or she isn't going to have a change of heart once the cat is out of the bag. Writers who don't like your pay rate are probably going to feel alienated if they find out what it is *after* they've already gone to the trouble to write a proposal. Let them know up front, so they don't waste their time (and yours).

Contact freelance writing websites

A list of some of the more popular places to list your guidelines is available in the appendix of this book. Usually, all you need to do is contact them with a link to your writer's guidelines. Some of them want you to fill out a form, but that generally just means cutting and pasting from information you already have.

You can get listed pretty easily in "Writer's Market," too, but you have to wait until you've actually published an issue. When you're ready to take this step, just email them at wmsupport@fwpubs.com and ask them to send you a publisher's questionnaire. Get this done as quickly as you can. It will take up to a year for your listing to appear in "Writer's Market," as it is only published annually.

Contracts

Always get signed contracts from your advertisers, writers, artists, and photographers. If you don't have a signed contract from each person who contributes to your magazine, you may be leaving yourself open to a lawsuit. A contract will protect you from misunderstandings and negligence on the part of your contributors.

A typical contract outlines the payment you owe to the contributor, what his or her obligations are, and how much you'll pay if you ultimately decide not to use the material. It is also a signed statement from the contributor that he or she is the copyright holder of the submitted material, and that he or she is releasing that material for your use. Additionally, if written correctly it will help protect you from libel lawsuits by placing the responsibility for libelous statements on the person who submitted the material.

I can't give you any legal advice on how to write these contracts. For this task, you need to consult a lawyer, who may charge you between $300 and $1,000 for each contract. This is a one-time fee, so think carefully before you decide to forego it. It will save you a lot of money if you ever run into any legal problems with material you have published.

Making money from potential writers

It may seem unfair to think along these lines, but potential writers can also be a source of revenue. After your first issue is on the newsstand, be sure you explicitly let freelancers know they should buy a copy before sending a proposal. As seedy as it sounds, this is actually a completely legitimate requirement. As a new publisher, you can't afford to give away free sample copies to every freelancer who is interested in sending you a poorly written proposal (as many of them will be). Anyone who is a serious freelancer knows that no writer should solicit a magazine without first reading a copy, simply because it's next to impossible to pitch an idea to a magazine you know nothing about. Writers need to see copies of a magazine in order to determine its voice and focus. The fact that this practice also happens to financially benefit you is a nice bonus. Everybody wins. The writer gets to find out what you're all about, and you'll have one less copy sitting in your garage.

Finding pictures

You can advertise for artists and photographers in much the same way as you advertise for writers, but the artistic type tends to be (at least in my experience) less able to accept working within your limited budget. Depending on your magazine's audience, you may have luck swapping advertising in exchange for photos and drawings, but if your readership isn't the type who you would generally expect to be interested in purchasing art or photography, this probably won't be adequate compensation.

Marketing departments

There are other ways to obtain images cheaply, though, so you don't have to feel like you're at the mercy of expensive photographers. Marketing departments, for example, are a great source of free images. Think carefully about how marketing images might be used in your magazine. For example, you may want to run an article in your cat magazine about cat toys. Rather than paying an expensive photographer to take pictures of cats playing with their toys, contact the manufacturers of cat toys and ask them if *they* have any pictures of cats playing with toys. Chances are, they will not only have photos they would be willing to let you use for free (in exchange for a photo credit and perhaps a mention in the sidebar that tells readers where they can buy cat toys), the photos will probably also be very high quality.

Be careful when using marketing photos, though, as you run the risk of making it look like your editorial content is influenced by your advertisers. This is something you always want to avoid. If readers believe you let your advertisers control your content, they're going to start questioning the objectivity and honesty of your writers. If the cat toys manufacturer gives you a photo of a cat sitting in front of a banner that says "Cats Love Acme Cat Toys," you probably want to avoid using that image. However, if it's just a picture of a cat playing with an Acme Cat Toy, you're probably OK using it.

Image brokers and the public domain

There are a number of companies that specialize in providing photographs to the media, and these tend to be less expensive than hiring professional photographers. You can also obtain "public domain" images from The Library of Congress, museums, and other archives. Be sure to check out the list of image brokers and public domain sources in the appendix of this book before you decide to hire a professional photographer or artist.

A word about copyright

Be very careful when you look for images from any source other than a professional photographer or artist (who will, presumably, sign a copyright release contract with you). Print publishers are particularly subject to copyright lawsuits. Be sure you have full permission from any source you've obtained an image from, or be sure that that image you're using is in the public domain. If you don't know, don't use the image. The appendix of this book lists a number of places where you can read about copyright law and the public domain. Be an expert on this subject before you attempt to use any images you don't have signed permission to reproduce.

To dummy or not to dummy?

You may have heard about the magazine "dummy," which other books have probably said you need to have before you can launch the real thing. A dummy issue is essentially a mock-up of what your magazine will look like when it's been printed. Basically, the dummy is designed to convince advertisers that they should buy ads in the premiere issue. It doesn't contain any real articles, ads, or any other content.

Again, unless you have a huge budget to throw at this project, printing a dummy is probably not going to be worth it to you. A dummy issue is going to cost at least as much to have printed as a regular issue, and a lot of advertisers want to see one or two real copies before they sign a contract anyway. Instead, consider your first issue to be your dummy issue. It will serve the same purpose as a dummy, but it will also have some value besides just acting as a marketing tool. You'll be able to sell your first issue to distributors and subscribers, which you wouldn't be able to do with a dummy.

Advertising

You should not try to sell advertising in your first issue. Chances are, your first issue isn't going to sell a lot of copies, so charging advertisers for placement just isn't very nice. If your budget depends on charging for advertising in your first issue, be prepared to give away a lot of free copies if you haven't sold as many as you anticipated by the time your next issue comes out. If you're following the established rules of publishing, your advertisers are paying you "per thousand," that is, if you told them 2,000 people will see their ad, you need to make sure 2,000 copies get into the hands of readers. If you don't think you're going to be able to do this with your first issue, don't charge anyone for ads.

Though you may cringe at the idea, giving away free advertising isn't completely without value. Be sure to give most of your free ads to advertisers who you think might eventually become paying customers. Almost no one will say "no" to a free ad, and your generous offer will do a couple of things for you. First, it will put you in the minds of the people who will most likely help you support your venture in the future. Second, it will make them feel like they owe you something. I've received a lot of mentions in newsletters, free ads on websites, offers for discounts on products and services, just based on a few free ads I gave away early in my magazine's life cycle.

Finally, all those ads you've given away for free make you look like the legitimate advertising vehicle you will eventually become. Put simply, ads make you look like a pro. Contrary to what you may think, people don't really prefer to see fewer ads. Advertising makes your readers feel like you are a professional quality publication, on a comparable level to the other magazines they buy at the newsstand. They will also make advertisers feel comfortable about buying ad space.

Pricing

So, how much should you charge for your magazine? You'll need to print the price on the cover; preferably, you should include both the U.S. and Canadian prices. Fortunately, this part is easy. Visit your local newsstand and figure out what magazines are in your basic genre. If your magazine is twice-yearly, try to find other twice-yearly magazines. Look at their cover prices and their subscription rates. Pay attention to how many pages are in each issue. Price your magazine based on that.

Layout

This is one subject that is strangely missing from almost every book I've seen on starting a magazine, yet it is one of the most important subjects new publishers need to know about. There are certain guidelines that you must follow when you are designing your new publication. Knowing what they are ahead of time will save you a lot of pain.

Software

You may already own a copy of Microsoft Publisher, and you may think, "why not just use this to design my magazine?" Sadly, you're thinking in the wrong direction. You can ask your printer if he or she will accept Publisher files, but your chances are pretty slim (though it never hurts to ask). Some printers will take files in PDF format, provided the software you're using will accomplish the translation well. Again, your printer can best explain if the software you're using is acceptable for creating PDFs. For most printers, though, there is only one standard: QuarkXpress.

Besides being the software preferred by most printers, Quark is also the industry standard. If you want to design a professional quality magazine, you need to use QuarkXpress. Unfortunately, though, Quark is not a cheap investment. A new copy will cost you around $800. If you shop around, you may be able to do better than this; I bought an old copy of Quark on eBay for around $125, then I had the registration transferred to my company's name and I upgraded to the new version for about $400. You have to be very careful doing this sort of thing, though. Be sure the used/old copy you're buying comes with the original books and box. You'll need these to transfer the registration into your name (otherwise Quark may think you're trying to register a pirated copy). The other problem with buying software on eBay is that a surprisingly large amount of it is pirated. Be sure you know what you're buying. Ask the seller for pictures of the CD, the box, books, or whatever. If you take all these precautions and you still wind up with a pirated copy, send the disk to Quark and contact your credit card company. Generally, your credit card company will reimburse you for the expense and go after the pirate in your stead.

You'll also need a copy of PhotoShop (which costs around $500). You may be able to get away with a cheaper image manipulation package, but PhotoShop gives you a lot of flexibility you don't have with other packages. Chances are, you'll need to do image retouching and scaling. If your package doesn't give you the ability to adjust DPI, color, and detail, you need to find something that does.

Color swatches

If you're going to be using color, you should buy a Pantone swatch, which generally costs about $100. Sometimes you can find these on eBay, but you won't usually save a lot of money by buying them this way. The purpose behind a Pantone swatch may seem a bit vague, but if you want to avoid the horror of badly reproduced color, this is not an expense you should snub.

In Quark, when you add color to a sidebar, a background, or a title, you should always select a Pantone color (consult your manual for details on how to do this). Then, compare the color you have selected to the color on your Pantone swatch. The chances are pretty good that it will look vastly different from the color on your screen. Always base your color selection on how the color looks on your Pantone swatch, no matter how wretched those colors may look on your screen. This is the only way you can be sure that the color will reproduce correctly. If you don't match your colors to Pantone colors, be prepared to be appalled when your proofs come back from the printer.

You'll need to know what kind of paper (coated or uncoated) you plan to use before buying your swatch. Colors will appear slightly different for each, and you'll have to use a different swatch. If in doubt, call your printer and ask which Pantone swatch you should buy.

Printer's specs

Printer's specs may vary from shop to shop, but in general:

If your magazine will have any colors or images that end at the edge of the page, you'll need to find out how your printer wants you to do "bleeds." Usually, this just means you need to extend the color or image beyond the physical edge of the page about 1/8th of an inch. Some printers have different requirements, so be sure to check.

Find out what resolution your printer wants images scanned at. If you don't know what dpi (dots per inch) your scanner defaults to, then you need to give yourself a crash course in image resolution. Almost all scanners default to 72dpi. This is web-ready resolution, but it doesn't work for magazines. Most printers require 300dpi for color photos, 200dpi for black and white.

You'll need to figure out how to adjust your scanner to the required dpi, and you need to make sure you always scan every image you submit to your printer at that resolution.

Convert all your color images to CMYK and convert all black and white images to grayscale. This can be done easily in PhotoShop, and your printer will undoubtedly require it.

Subscription cards

Be sure to design a subscription card, which you should always include with every copy of your magazine. There are several schools of thought on the best way to do this. The first is to have one or two cards stitched into each magazine. This is the least expensive way to do things, and it guarantees that every copy will give someone the opportunity to become a subscriber. The other way to do it is with "blow-ins." Blow-ins are the annoying little cards that float out of every magazine you've ever taken off the newsstand. They are the things that end up all over your floor whenever you read the latest copy of any publication. They are designed to make it very easy for someone to subscribe; because they don't have to be torn from the inside of the magazine, a potential subscriber can throw one in with a stack of bills and pay it with the rest of the outgoing expenses. And because he or she has 15 copies of the same card scattered all over the house, he or she isn't likely to forget to put that little card in the mail.

Making it official

BIPAD

Another thing a new publisher absolutely must have is a BIPAD number. This is the number that appears on the UPC code in the bottom corner of your magazine's cover. If you want to sell your magazine on the newsstand (and believe me, you do), you'll need to obtain one of these

UPC codes. Most distributors will not deal with a magazine that doesn't have a UPC.

Relax, it isn't as intimidating as it sounds. It does require an initial investment of about $300, but after that one-time fee your UPC will cost just $35 each issue. To obtain your BIPAD number, go to www.bipad.com and download the application form. You can either fax it to BIPAD, or send it by surface mail.

After you've received your BIPAD number, you'll need to buy a UPC. This is handled by a company called Product Identification and Processing Systems Inc. (PIPS). For information about obtaining a UPC, visit www.pips.com/pi.htm. At the time of this writing, PIPS didn't have an online ordering mechanism, but if you complete their contact form (www.pips.com/contact.htm) they'll send you the information you need to place your order. The UPC can be sent electronically, and will usually arrive just hours after you've purchased it. PIPS will also send you instructions on how to add the image to the cover of your magazine. The instructions are very specific, so be sure to read them carefully.

ISSN

Like books, all magazines have a special number that uniquely identifies them to libraries, bookstores, or any other organization that archives or catalogs publications. In books this number is the ISBN; in magazines it is the ISSN (International Standard Serial Number). You don't *need* one—that is, no regulation *requires* it, but having one will benefit you. First of all, it will lend credibility to your publication (it will make you look like a *real* magazine). Second, it will make it possible for libraries to archive your magazine. The best reason why you should do it, though, is because it is easy and it doesn't actually cost you anything.

An ISSN is assigned by the U.S. Library of Congress. You can download the application from the L.O.C. website (lcweb.loc.gov/issn/), where you can also read up on the ins and outs of ISSN, or you can write to:

> **Library of Congress**
> National Serials Data Program
> 101 Independence Avenue, SE
> Washington, D.C. 20540-4160
> (202) 707-6452
> issn@loc.gov

You should obtain your ISSN as quickly as possible—before your first issue goes to the printer.

Registering for copyright protection

Federal law automatically assigns copyright protection to your magazine and its content. Technically, you don't have to do anything to secure this protection—but you can take steps that will make it easier for you to defend your copyright claim should the need arise.

You should register each issue of your magazine with U.S. Copyright Office, so there will always be an official record of who produced the work and who therefore owns the copyright. To do this, visit the U.S. Copyright Office's website (www.copyright.gov/register/serial.html), download the appropriate form, and follow the three-step instructions. Or, write to:

> **Library of Congress**
> Copyright Office
> 101 Independence Avenue, S.E.
> Washington, D.C. 20559-6000

Chapter 4: After you've gone to press

Preparing for ad and subscription sales

Now you've got a little time to breathe. But you can use this downtime productively by marketing heavily to potential subscribers and advertisers, so by the time your magazine comes back from the printer you'll already have orders to fill.

Start billing people

While your magazine is at the printer, send bills to everyone who "reserved" a subscription on your website. Don't make the same mistake I did by mailing each of these people a copy of the magazine and trusting that they will all pay you. Most people won't. They are far too used to "free trial issue" offers, and many of them assume that every first issue is a free trial issue, whether the magazine explicitly said it was or not. As a new magazine with a low budget, you should never send anyone a copy on the honor system. Postage is too expensive, and you paid way too much money for each of those copies that you're trustingly mailing off to complete strangers.

Include a survey with your invoices. You want to start learning about your audience as early as you can. Ask them their age group, income level, buying habits, etc. Choose questions that would particularly interest potential advertisers. For example, your model airplane magazine will appeal to advertisers who are in the model airplane manufacturing business. Ask your subscribers how many new model planes they buy every month. Ask them if they would be interested in airplane art, books, museums, etc. Ask them if they'll be likely to share copies of your magazine with friends. Anything that will give your advertisers an idea about who your audience is (and how many of them there are) will help you sell ads. You'd be surprised at how many people will take the time to fill out a survey. Most of them will. People like to fill out surveys, as long as they're not too overwhelming (don't make them any longer than, say, 2/3rds of a page).

Your subscriber database

Because you are selling subscriptions (vs. items you only have to mail once), you need an extremely accurate database system. Ideally you will want to use database software such as Microsoft Access for this, because database software is extremely good at keeping track of who has paid you, how many issues they have remaining on their subscription, when they should be contacted for renewal, etc. You may need to purchase a database template if you don't know how to build one of your own. The Independent Press Association (www.indypress.org) has a database template (which is only available to members) that works in FileMaker Pro, or you can buy an Access template from Palfrey Media (www.palfreymedia.com).

If you want to have a stab at building your own database, make sure it can keep track of the following information:

1. Basic contact info (name, address, phone, email)
2. Country and Post Code (if you plan to sell internationally)
3. Price paid
4. How many issues received
5. How many issues remaining
6. Paid/unpaid
7. Type of customer (subscriber, single issue, gift subscription)
8. Status (active subscriber, cancelled subscriber, postal return, expired, returned subscription)
9. Starting issue date

10. Ending issue date
11. List rental yes/no
12. Step renewals yes/no
13. Notes

Create your media kit

You need to have a media kit in order to help sell your magazine to potential advertisers. This is basically a classy-looking folder that holds a current copy of your magazine, an order form, and some basic information about your magazine and its advertising policies, including:

1. **Your editorial/mission statement**
2. **Where you plan to distribute your magazine**
    If your magazine will only be distributed locally, say so. If you only plan to market in a couple of states for the time being, say so. Be totally honest about what your plans are—even if they aren't that ambitious just yet.
3. **Mechanical requirements**
    What sizes will your ads be? In general, magazines sell full page, 2/3rds page, 1/2 page, 1/3 page, 1/4 page, 1/6 page, and 1/8 page ads. Some will sell ads by column inch. It is up to you to let your advertisers know the exact measurements for each of these sizes. To do this, open up a magazine with the same trim size as yours, and measure each of their ad sizes.
4. **Prices/rates**
    Your highest priced ad will be your back cover, with the two inside covers next, followed by full page ads. Color ads are, of course, more expensive than black and white. See "Pricing your ads" below for information on establishing fair ad rates.
5. **Demographics**
    In the early stages, you won't really know your demographics. As subscription invoices are returned to you, you will be able to make estimates based on the answers to your survey,

but because you probably won't have any significant numbers to go by you won't really be able to say anything for sure. Just make sure you let potential advertisers know that you don't have solid statistics and are making a guess. Say something like, "we expect our subscribers will be well-educated, in the 35-50 age group," etc.).

6. **Terms and conditions**

This is generally a separate fact sheet, which gives advertisers instructions on how they should submit ads to you. It should contain the following information:

    1. **File format**

You will need to let your advertisers know what software they should use to build their ads. Obviously, you don't want them to send you files you can't open. Just list the programs you currently use (QuarkXpress, PhotoShop, etc.) and the file formats each program reads (usually TIF, PDF, and EPS). Make sure advertisers know that image files must be 300dpi. Ask them not to send GIFs or JPGs; these files have been compressed for the web and are no good for print.

    2. **Color**

If an advertiser sends you an image that isn't CMYK, you can always convert it yourself—but it's usually wise to have them do it for you since the color may look different after the conversion.

    3. **Fonts**

If the advertiser is sending an ad in Quark or a similar layout program, you'll need to remind them to also send any fonts they used with the design. Take care—if you have a PC and they have a Mac, your fonts won't be compatible. You'll need to ask them to convert the image to a TIF before you'll be able to use it.

    4. **Media**

Do you have a Zip drive, or do images

need to be sent on CD? Do you have an FTP site where advertisers can upload images? Or do you prefer to scan everything in-house? You'll need to outline this so your advertiser knows how to get his or her ad to you.

5. **Terms**

   Here's the legal stuff, where you absolve yourself from responsibility if you have to redesign an ad, if you don't print it for whatever reason, or if you make a mistake in processing the ad request. You should also make it clear that the advertiser accepts all responsibility for the content of his or her ad. Talk to a lawyer if you need to know the correct way to author this section.

6. **Billing**

   Let advertisers know how they will be billed. Consider requiring all first-time advertisers to pay in advance. Let them know how much interest they will have to pay if they don't pay on time.

Pricing your ads

How much should you charge? That's the $64,000 question. Unfortunately, you can't just pick up a similarly priced magazine on a similar topic and use their ad rates. Advertisers expect to pay based on CPM, or "cost per thousand"—so unless you know you're going to have a circulation of, say, 40,000 right out of the gate, you can't realistically expect to base your prices on those of a similar magazine that has a circulation of 40,000. Instead, you need to base your prices on 2,000 copies, or whatever you *think* your circulation will be. And as I've said, if you don't sell as many copies as you promised your advertisers you would, you must give the rest of them away. So lowball your figures if you want to be safe.

CPM works like this: a magazine with a circulation of 5,000 that charges $500 for a full-page ad has a CPM of $100 for that size ad ($100 for every 1,000 readers).

Depending on how exclusive your audience is, you can charge as little as $2 or $3 per 1,000 or $300 or $400 per 1,000. In general, magazines that appeal to a very specific, exclusive audience (CEOs who play golf, for example) can charge a lot more for their ads. Magazines that appeal to a more general audience (people who live in the Western half of the United States, for example) don't get to charge as much. The CPM for an audited publication (one that has had its circulation independently verified by an outside agency) is also typically higher than it is for an unaudited publication (like yours).

The best way to determine CPM is to pick up a magazine that has similar content and a similar circulation to your own, then set a CPM that is about 2/3rds of what theirs is. That way, you're giving your potential advertisers a reason to leave the publications they're already advertising with—they're saving money, but they're still getting the same amount of exposure.

Accepting credit cards

You've got to have a merchant account. If you're not accepting credit cards, you're passing up a huge opportunity for potential sales, especially from Internet shoppers. Internet shoppers are notorious for buying stuff on impulse. If you don't give them an easy way to do this, they'll take their impulse somewhere else. Accepting credit cards online is the single most profitable way you'll sell your magazine. By selling single issues and subscriptions on your website, you'll avoid having to sacrifice a substantial percentage of each sale to a distributor or retailer. To put it bluntly, you must accept credit cards or die.

"Traditional" merchant accounts

Having said that, merchant accounts are expensive. I don't recommend signing up for a traditional merchant account unless you're already getting a lot of traffic to your website (say 20,000 visits a month) and a lot of subscription reservations. The reason is because you'll end up paying a lot of what many people affectionately refer to as "hidden charges." So what a merchant account service advertises probably will look on the surface to be a lot cheaper than what it actually is.

One of these typical merchant account services will usually charge you somewhere between 2.19 percent and 2.29 percent of each transaction, plus a 25¢ to 30¢ service charge per transaction. But some services will also charge you application and setup fees, gateway fees (a charge for electronically submitting a transaction) and some will require a monthly minimum (for example, if you accrue less than $50 in charges one month, you'll have to pay $50 anyway).

It is easy enough to find merchant accounts that don't have setup fees and minimums, so be sure to ask before you sign up. If you know you're going to sell a lot of copies right away, then go ahead and sign up for one of these traditional accounts, because you will save money in the long run.

If you're pretty sure you're going to be low volume for a while, you might want to try a different option. There are a couple of credit card services that specialize in helping low-volume businesses (and hence don't charge high monthly service charges or other hidden fees), but they don't tend to be practical for magazines because they will typically charge higher per-transaction fees. If you're selling single copies of your magazine at $3.95 each, you don't want to have to pay 70¢ for every transaction plus whatever percentage of the sale you'll have to pay to the service.

Third party payment processors

For a new magazine looking to save money, this type of service may be the best way to go. A third party payment processor is essentially a middle-man. It acts as the merchant by processing the transaction and then emailing you with the order. So a third party processor will generally take a higher percentage of each transaction than a traditional merchant account will, but you won't have to worry about monthly spending minimums or high account fees. When choosing a third party payment processor, you'll need to shop around, because charges vary wildly (some third party services will charge more than $1 per transaction, or as much as 20 percent of every sale). A list of some of the more reasonably priced services appears in the appendix to this book.

One of the drawbacks to using a third party processor is that it makes your website look somewhat unprofessional. When a customer adds your magazine to his or her "shopping cart" and then checks out, they leave your site altogether and go to the third party processor's page, which will look completely different from where they came from. This can (and probably will) scare away some of your potential customers, who may perceive the transaction as being less secure. Just be aware that this sort of thing may happen, and make an educated decision on how you want to handle the credit card question.

I've got 5,000 copies in my garage, now what?

After your magazine arrives, go out for an evening on the town. You've earned it. The next day, though, be ready to get back to work. The clock is ticking. Book publishers have the luxury of time—they can sell copies of the same book years after its publication date. Your magazine, on the other hand, has a limited shelf life. You need to sell as many copies as you can before it's time to replace the old issue with a new one.

Magazine distributors

Before you do anything, sign up with as many distributors as will have you. This is one of the big mistakes I personally made when I started my first magazine. I believed that I could sell more copies on my own, and thus save myself the 55% discount that is the industry standard for magazine distribution. As it turned out, I would have been much better off taking the 55% cut.

First, here's what you can expect from distribution. You will receive about 45% of the cover cost of your magazine from your distributors. If your magazine has a cover price of $4.95, this means you'll only actually see $2.23 for every copy sold.

Unfortunately, every copy will not sell. 50% is considered an average "sell-through" rate, so for every 100 magazines you send to your distributor, you'll probably only see about $111.50. Worse, the magazines that don't sell may not even come back to you in one piece. Retailers aren't required to pay for magazines they don't sell. Instead, they can return them to the distributor for a full refund. Sometimes they send them back whole, sometimes they just send the covers—which means that you will not only lose what it cost you to have each of those magazines printed, you'll also lose the ability to sell them as "back issues" after the next issue comes out.

So, you are probably asking, why bother with distributors at all? Well, there are a couple of very good reasons. The first is because the $111.50 you get for 100 magazines that got as far as the newsstand is far better than the $0 you'll get for 100 magazines that are still sitting in your garage. You will not be able to sell all those magazines on your website. It's just not logistically possible unless you are Primedia or Time Warner.

The second reason is because selling single issues isn't really the main goal of distribution. You're not trying to earn a lot of money this way; what you're really trying to do is attract new subscribers. Single-issue sales are the best way to turn people into paid subscribers. Though some publishers will tout promotional (free) copies in the same way, I don't think they have nearly the same kind of return (I once got three subscribers out of a promotional giveaway of 400 copies). The problem with giving magazines away for free is that most people will take a copy just based on it being free. They don't even have to be interested in it. The word "free" is like a magical elixir. Have you ever been given a free t-shirt that you didn't really like, but just couldn't turn down because, hey, "it's free?"

A person who has paid for a magazine, though, is a different sort of prospect. If they've gone to the trouble to stand in line, dig $4.95 plus tax from their wallet, and walk the magazine up to the checkout, chances are they're interested in it. They'll read it, and if they like it, they may even subscribe.

With that in mind, go to the list of distributors that appears in the appendix of this book. Most of these distributors specialize in independently published magazines, but it will behoove you to visit their websites (if they have them) and find out exactly what sorts of magazines they carry. For example, some specialize only in literary journals, and some will only distribute magazines that appear four times a year or more. Don't waste your postage on distributors that aren't a good fit.

After you've narrowed down the list to those distributors who you think might be interested in your magazine, mail your latest issue and a letter of introduction to each one. Include a self-addressed stamped envelope to encourage them to reply to you. Do this while your magazine is still warm. Sometimes it takes weeks (or longer) to receive a reply. Ideally, you want to sign on with as many distributors as you can before your next issue becomes available.

Most distributors will start with small orders (100 to 150 copies), so the more distributors you can get the better off you will be. Just make sure you let each distributor know the names of other distributors you are working with, so they don't step on each others' toes. Distributors can sometimes get a bit catty over who gets to sell to what bookstore or newsstand.

Non-traditional outlets

Non-traditional outlets like specialty shops are surprisingly hard to crack. For example, your model airplane magazine may seem like a natural fit for the hobby shop down the road, but you'll have to work hard to get that shop to show an interest. If you can manage to get onto their shelves, you'll be in an ideal position. Everyone who approaches your magazine on their newsstand will be a potential reader, with interests that are in line with your subject matter. Also, because you'll avoid using a distributor, you'll be able to collect up to 65% of your cover price for each issue sold.

The great difficulty of breaking into a non-traditional outlet is getting the shop owner to pay attention to your solicitations. In general, small business owners often just can't be bothered to put a lot of effort into selling a specific magazine, because magazines just don't generate a lot of income compared to the bigger-ticket items they regularly sell. I tried a couple of different approaches towards getting into non-traditional outlets, and was never particularly successful. That doesn't mean you can't be. I'm not a very good salesman, and in order to do this well you need to have a salesman's persistence.

Here are a couple of suggestions on how you might approach this challenge:

1. **Do some research**
   Go to one of the major yellow pages websites (like www.superpages.com) and look up shops that might be interested in carrying your magazine. Check every state. This will take some time, but it's still much quicker than doing the same thing with the yellow pages at your local

library. Build a database (or just an Excel spreadsheet) that holds the addresses and telephone numbers of every shop you think might want to carry your magazine.

2. **Don't bother with direct mail**
I sent out loads of postcards to shops that catered exclusively to my readers. In return, I got one phone call, and one order. Definitely not worth the money. Most retailers get tons of this kind of junk mail, and it goes directly in to the trash—right along with the 42¢ you spent having it printed, and the 23¢ stamp you had to put on it.

3. **Pick up the telephone**
I hate doing this. Probably this is one of the many things that contributed to my downfall. But I still believe it is the best way to break into a non-traditional outlet. Despite the loathing a lot of people have for telemarketers, shop owners are much more likely to show an interest in your product if you take the time to call them. Don't think of it as telemarketing—you're not calling them at home at dinner time. You're calling them at their place of business, asking them a legitimate business question.

4. **Offer to give them something for free**
Buy them a magazine rack they can put next to their cash register. This has the double bonus of making them feel as if they're getting something for nothing, and putting you in the best possible location in their shop (right at the checkout line, where a customer will be most likely to pick up your magazine).

5. **Don't be afraid to use email**
Chances are, you won't get a huge return if you contact retailers by email. But it doesn't cost you anything to do, so why not give it a try? Just avoid making it look like "spam." Personalize each message by addressing it to the shop owner or by including the name of the store. If a recipient thinks you're just another piece of junk email, they're likely to delete your message without even reading it. It's important to make your message look as personal as you can.

6. **If you're short on cash ...**
   Start by soliciting shops in your area. The
   advantage of doing this is that you can go down
   there in person and talk to the shop owner
   yourself. You can also offer to come pick up
   unsold copies and deliver the new issue
   personally. That way, the retailer doesn't have to
   worry about the shipping costs on return copies.
   It is a no-risk situation for them, and there's no
   reason why they shouldn't say "yes." Make sure
   they know this.

Agreeing on the specifics

The cost of getting your magazines to the retailer is
something you can always negotiate. As a general rule,
make it as simple for the retailer as you can. I always
sent copies COD, and I picked up the cost of shipping to
the retailer's location. In return, the retailer had to pay
shipping on returned copies (which gave them an extra
incentive to sell the copies rather than have to return
them). I always asked retailers to return whole
magazines instead of covers. Some retailers will object to
this policy; it's up to you if you want to eat the cost of
unsold magazines or insist that they be returned in one
piece.

Subscription brokers

Don't bother. These are places like www.amazon.com
and www.magazania.com, which look great in theory but
will end up costing you a ton of money in the long run.
Most of these houses pay an abysmal 10% or less to the
publisher, and they handle all the renewals of each
subscription sold, so you won't even have a chance to
earn a full subscription price when renewal time comes
around. The only publishers that benefit from
subscription brokers are large houses that depend on
advertising for all or most of their revenue. Basically,
selling on Amazon.com or Magazania.com is simply a
way to add to your circulation numbers, so you can up
your advertising rates. Unless your magazine is super-

mass-marketed, you'll never do anything but lose money with this kind of distribution.

Chapter 5: Marketing

You must market aggressively

This is another mistake a lot of new publishers make.
Your website is an inexpensive way to market your
magazine, but it is not going to be enough. You need to
do some traditional advertising as well.

Seeking advertisers

Now is the time to start finding advertisers for your next
issue. As soon as your issue comes back from the printer,
start contacting people you think might be interested in
advertising. Small businesses will be your most likely
candidates. Big companies like Ford or American
Airlines aren't going to waste their time and money on a
little publication with a circulation of 2,000, so don't
bother going after the big accounts for a while. Small
businesses will be much more likely to be in search of an
inexpensive advertising vehicle, which makes your
magazine the perfect choice for them.

Direct mail can work with advertisers, but in my opinion
there is nothing better than a phone call. Pick up a
magazine that is similar to yours, and start contacting
that magazine's advertisers, particularly those that have
placed classified ads or smaller black and white ads
(those are the folks who have the right budget for your
magazine). That seems a bit sleazy, I know, but people
who are already familiar with magazine advertising are
going to be a lot more receptive to the idea of advertising
in your magazine than someone you found in the white
pages.

Send anyone who is interested a free copy of your
magazine and a media kit. Be sure to follow up with a

phone call. Offer reluctant people a discount on their first ad. Offer the first ad for free if they agree to buy another ad in a subsequent issue. Do anything you can to hook them.

You can also find potential advertisers by searching the Internet. Look for people who have category listings on Yahoo! (Yahoo! charges for category listings, so a business that has invested in a Yahoo! listing is generally going to be one that already has an advertising budget). Also look for businesses that have well-designed websites. A well-designed website is an indication of a serious business, and a person who is serious about his or her business is much more likely to be in the market for advertising than someone who has a fly-by-night Geocities website.

Again, when you contact potential advertisers by email, be sure to personalize your message. Mention some of their products by name, for example, and address the business owner by name. The more personal you make your message, the less it will look like spam, making its recipient much more likely to read it.

Hiring a sales rep

If you're no good at cold calling and you can't stand rejection, you might want to consider hiring someone to help you sell ads. If you're low budget, you should look into hiring someone on commission only. Be sure to check your local employment laws and tax codes to find out how you can do this legally. This is another area I can't give you any advice on—that's a completely different book. Be sure to buy it.

Chances are this is not going to be a full time job for anyone. Until you have a substantial subscriber base, your sales rep isn't going to sell enough ads at your low ad rate to afford to feed his or her family. Advertise your sales rep opportunity as a part-time "extra cash" kind of thing. Don't expect anyone to devote a whole workweek to it. If possible, hire a friend or even a college student who is studying advertising.

Seeking subscribers

There are a lot of schools of thought on how to get new subscribers. You'll hear people refer to your subscriber pool as a "leaking bucket," which essentially means you'll be losing subscribers almost as fast as you'll be attracting new ones. Subscribers are a fickle lot. Some will subscribe to your magazine only to decide later that it's not really what they're looking for. Some will just decide they don't have time to read it. Some will decide they can't afford it. Some will just forget to send in their renewal. So all the time you're gaining new subscribers, you're losing old ones. The trick is to attract more subscribers than you are losing.

Direct mail

A lot of small publishers will tell you that direct mail is still the best way to get new subscribers. This may be true, but direct mail is also very expensive. In addition to mailing list rental fees (which, as I've said, probably cost you a minimum of $1,250), you'll have to pay for printing costs, design fees (unless you decide to design the mailing yourself), and postage. And unless you are mass mailing, your return is going to be pretty small. 1% is considered average; anything higher than that is astoundingly good. So if you send a mailing to 5,000 people, you can expect to get 50 new subscribers.

Card deck advertising

Card deck advertising is a form of direct mail, but it tends to be less expensive per-piece than traditional direct mail. If you've never received a card deck ad, it's essentially a stack of 3x5 cards containing various offers that are targeted to your interests. There are tons of card decks specializing in just about every kind of personal interest.

Card deck advertising is also less of a headache than traditional direct mail. If you buy a card deck ad, you only have to worry about the ad's design. You don't have to worry about postage, address labels, printing, or any of the other expenses that go along with the ad. You may pay as little as 2¢ or 3¢ per household for your ad, and the decks may go to 500,000 households or more. Overall, it's a relatively large investment for any low-budget publication (I paid $2,000 for a card deck ad that went to 100,000 people), but the return on your investment is probably going to be a lot higher than it will be from a traditional direct mail campaign.

Email marketing

As I've already mentioned, email marketing is not always bad. You can use it to attract advertisers, and you can also use it to attract subscribers. Choose a double opt-in email list, like you did when you conducted your magazine's initial survey. This is an inexpensive alternative to direct mail. Your return probably won't be as high, but the chances are you'll get more for your money.

You can also email people you've found on the Internet, especially people who have posted to newsgroups or have personal websites on your topic with "contact me" links. When you market this way, though, you must be very careful. You are treading a very fine line between legitimate email marketing and "spamming." Many people don't object to highly targeted email marketing, but some will consider any sort of unsolicited email to be spam, targeted or not. You should decide for yourself whether or not you want to take this kind of risk. You may be "blacklisted" if someone decides you're a spammer, which could jeopardize your contract with your Internet service provider, or, worse, give you a bad name in your industry.

If you do decide to pursue unsolicited emailing as a marketing technique, there are ways to be clever about it. Contact people who have listed classified ads on free classified websites, and offer them a free classified ad in your magazine. I actually got subscribers by doing this, though only a handful of them. People do respond well to "free" offers, and ads don't really cost you anything to give away.

Web marketing

Buy banner ads, stay on top of your search engine listings, and keep looking for new websites where you can post a link to your website. Buy banner ads periodically and study your results. Internet advertising is one of the cheapest ways to get the word out about your magazine.

Once your first issue is on the newsstands, you can also turn to Internet newsgroups for another inexpensive form of advertising. Just be careful to understand the "spamming" rules of each group before you post anything. Some groups don't mind advertising, as long as it is on-topic. Others forbid any advertising of any kind. In particular, look for groups that cover subjects you tackled in your current issue. Then just post a little note to the group letting them know they can read about the subject in the latest issue of your magazine. Include a link to your current issue page, and a link to your order page.

Other magazines

I put off advertising in other magazines for a long time. This was another big mistake. I was afraid other magazines would refuse to print my ad (because I was essentially a competing publication), so I didn't even bother asking. After all, why would any publication want to run a competitor's ad?

You may run into this problem with some publications, but for the most part, as long as your magazine isn't a carbon copy of the one you want to advertise in, most publications aren't going to turn down your money. Other magazines are a great place to advertise. A small ad doesn't generally cost a lot, and it has the potential to produce a lot of qualified leads. For one thing, you are marketing your magazine to the exact group of people you want to reach: magazine readers who have an interest in your subject matter. Don't dismiss this advertising possibility. It's far too valuable to overlook.

Be creative

There are a lot of imaginative ways to advertise your magazine. There are also a lot of cheap ways to do it. Have a brainstorming session and write down every idea that comes to your mind. Think about the magazines you subscribe to, or the ones you have subscribed to in the past. How were you introduced to those magazines? Did you see an ad somewhere? What about that ad attracted you to the magazine? Advertise in any way you think might get people interested in your product. Put a bumper sticker on your car. Put a magnetic sign on your car. Put up flyers in shops and leave stacks of them at events that cater to your potential audience. Take copies to local doctors and dentists and ask if you can leave them in the waiting room. Sponsor local events. Donate copies to fundraisers (a lot of non-profit organizations will compensate you for this by giving you free ad space in their event program or their newsletter). There are lots of ways to advertise on the cheap. Take advantage of as many of them as you can.

A word about "trial issues"

You may think giving away free trial issues is a normal and natural way to attract new subscribers. I disagree. Never, ever, ever offer anyone a free trial issue. This is a marketing technique for the big players, magazines that have some serious cash to throw at their marketing plan and are the lucky recipients of the post office's periodicals rate. I wasted thousands of dollars doing this. It was the single biggest mistake I made as a new publisher.

Why is it such a bad investment? Because most people believe that magazine publishers are rolling around in piles of cash. They will order the free trial of your magazine just because it is free. They have absolutely no thought for your financial situation, no concern for whether or not your magazine lives or dies, and absolutely no sense of empathy for you as an independent publisher. As far as they are concerned, you can afford to send them the free issue just based on the fact that you are a magazine publisher, and you are therefore rolling around in piles of cash. The sad truth is, most people who take advantage of the free trial issue offer don't have any intention of evaluating the magazine to see if it is something they would like to subscribe to, which is supposed to be the intent of the offer. Most have no intention of ever subscribing. They just want the free issue. You are throwing your money away if you pursue this kind of marketing campaign. Trust me, don't do it.

The same goes for including a "bill me" option on your subscription card. You can do this, but don't send anyone an issue before you've been paid. The "free trial issue" precedent is too common in our industry, and you'll lose money if you send out subscription orders on the honor system—especially since your magazine is probably not going to look like the magazines people are used to seeing. Because they are so used to getting a free trial issue of every magazine they subscribe to, people who decide they don't like your magazine before they've paid for it may feel like it's OK to keep the first issue and throw the bill away.

It's an ugly truth that a lot of people will be disappointed in your magazine. Don't take this personally. People who are used to seeing mass-market publications are going to expect something that looks like Newsweek—at least 96 pages, lots of ads, and a certain "look and feel." Because your magazine isn't going to meet the standards of most mass-marketed publications (it may not be 100% color, it may be much shorter, it may only have a few ads), some people are going to reject it based on visual appeal alone. It is not up to you to eat the cost of your first issue just because someone has decided that he or she doesn't like the way it looks. If that person has placed an order and you have fulfilled your part of the bargain by filling their order, they need to fulfill their obligation by paying you. If they wanted to evaluate a copy first, they should have ordered a single issue. You're not in the business of paying people to read your magazine, which is essentially what you'll be doing if you send new subscriptions out on the honor system.

Hang in there

A final piece of advice, or perhaps just a reiteration of what I've already said: don't do more than you can afford. Your small budget limits how much of a bang you can make with your first couple of issues, so set a budget you know you can stick to for a long time, then grow as your readership grows. Slow growth is healthy, and it will give you more time to succeed.

Good luck!

Appendix A: How much is this gonna cost me?

Before you decide to dive in to the independent publishing industry, I think it's essential for you to know the bare minimum you will need to spend in order to get started. If you don't have enough capital to invest in these startup costs, you may want to work on saving a little money before you begin.

Required expenses		
Item	*Minimum Price*	*Maximum Price*
Computer with CD-RW	$599	$4,645
Laser printer	$119	$2,599
Scanner with negative and slide scanning ability	$99	$1,056
QuarkXpress	$599 (version 4.1)	$789 (latest version)
PhotoShop	$499 (version 6)	$599 (latest version)
Pantone swatch	$99	$99
Postage scale	$28	$185
Domain name	$8/year	$35/year
Web hosting	$9/month	$35/month

Business telephone line	$15/month	$29/month
Merchant account or third party payment processor	PayPal: 2.9% + 30¢ per transaction CCNow: 9% + $9.99/month	$395 account setup, 2.25% + 25¢ per transaction, $10 statement fee, $25 transaction fee, $25 monthly minimum
Pre-printed envelopes	$74/500 black & white	$400/500 color
Business cards	$24/500 black & white	$85/500 color
BIPAD number	$300 application fee	--
Barcode	$35/issue	--

Optional but highly recommended expenses

Item	Minimum Price	Maximum Price
Stamps.com account	$4.49/month + 10% service fee	$15.99/month
Overture.com pay per click account	$25/month minimum	$Unlimited

Printing

Printing is your largest single required expense. This is one area it really pays to shop around in. Following are some example rates you can expect to pay for 5,000 copies of various lengths/color/paper stock—but this list is by no means a standard and it doesn't include extra costs like a subscription card insert, using a heavier paper stock for the cover, and stitching (stapling the magazine together). Costs will vary wildly. Be sure you get an estimate in writing, and be sure your printer includes things like shipping, pre-press charges (if any), and the cost of last-minute changes (these are changes you make after the proofs come back to you, which can be excessive and surprising if you aren't prepared for them).

Paper Stock	Number of Pages	Number of pages with color	Price
#50 coated	8	8 BW	$460
#60 coated	8	8 BW	$495
#50 coated	8	4 color/4 BW	$660
#60 coated	8	4 color/4 BW	$695
#50 coated	8	8 color	$855
#60 coated	8	8 color	$895
#50 coated	16	16 BW	$775
#60 coated	16	16 BW	$840

#50 coated	16	8 color/8 BW	$1,095
#60 coated	16	8 color/8 BW	$1,165
#50 coated	16	16 color	$1,420
#60 coated	16	16 color	$1,495
#50 coated	32	32 BW	$1,550
#60 coated	32	32 BW	$1,680
#50 coated	32	16 color/16 BW	$2,195
#60 coated	32	16 color/16 BW	$2,335
#50 coated	32	32 color	$2,840
#60 coated	32	32 color	$2,990
#50 coated	48	48 BW	$2,325
#60 coated	48	48 BW	$2,520
#50 coated	48	16 color/32 BW	$2,970
#50 coated	48	32 color/16 BW	$3,615
#60 coated	48	16 color/32 BW	$3,175
#60 coated	48	32 color/16 BW	$3,830
#50 coated	48	48 color	$4,260
#60 coated	48	48 color	$4,485

(These figures are based on a 2002 printing quote. Be aware that printing prices change all the time, and depending on the current market you may or may not be able to find a printer who can match these prices.)

Appendix B: Publisher's essential resources

Domain registration

There are loads of places where you can buy domain names for cheap. Don't go to Network Solutions or any of the big name services; you'll end up paying $35 a year. Not necessary. Try one of these services for discounted domain registration. Be sure to do your own search for domain registrars, too, as prices are changing all the time.

BuyDomains www.buydomains.com	**Namesecure** www.namesecure.com
Go Daddy Software registrar.godaddy.com	**registerfly** www.registerfly.com

Web hosting

Web hosting can be done cheaply, too. Just be sure you know what you need. For example, if you want a form mailer (and you will if you want to accept subscription reservations or if you want to conduct surveys) you will need site hosting that supports ASP, JSP or CGI, and you will need to know how to implement these tools on your website. If your knowledge of web programming is limited, choose a service that has good customer support, free website utilities, and lots of FAQs.

I will not attempt to list web hosting companies here; there are way too many to choose from. Instead, I am

72

providing the URLs to four services that will help you
compare the features of various web hosting companies.
Again, exercise caution when choosing your provider.
They are not all created equal. My advice is to be sure
your hosting provider offers a money back guarantee, so
you can back out if you don't like what they have to offer,
or if you find you're in over your head.

AceHosts.com www.acehosts.com	**HostChart.com** www.hostchart.com
CompareWebHosts.com www.comparewebhosts.com	**HostIndex.com** www.hostindex.com

HTML tutorials

If you don't already know HTML, there are plenty of
websites that can help you learn. Although tools like
FrontPage and other similar editors can be useful for the
beginner, you can save yourself a lot of headache in the
long run by learning how to "hand-code." It's not
difficult and it won't take you long to master. Following
are a few of the more useful HTML tutorials:

HTML: An Interactive Tutorial for Beginners
www.davesite.com/webstation/html
(Beware the pop-ups. They are
unusually excessive.)

The Bare Bones Guide to HTML
werbach.com/barebones

HTML Primer
www.htmlprimer.com

How To Create A Web Page
www.make-a-web-site.com

Building a contact form for your website

Your website will need a contact form, which is not something that HTML knows how to do by itself. I have included below the basic code for a "form mailer," that is, a form that will email you with the information a visitor enters into it. In order for this form to work you will need an ASP capable hosting package (check with your hosting company to make sure you do). You can use this code for surveys, subscription reservations, or to collect any other kind of information from a user. Just be sure you have a privacy policy on your website that lets your visitors know how you plan to use this information (especially if you are going to send them any marketing material or you think you might one day "rent" your subscriber list to other companies).

Copy the following code as-is into a blank "Notepad" document and name it "contactform.asp". Pay special attention to areas marked in gray. These are the areas you'll need to change in order for the code to work properly. Other than that, don't alter anything unless you know something about ASP.

```
<html>
<head>

<%
Dim Action
Action = Request.Form("Action")

If Action = "Submit" Then
        Call Submit()
End If
%>

<%
Sub Submit()
```

```
%>

<%

Dim Body
Dim Mail
Dim Email

'*****************************************
'*** In the space below (after "Dim"),
'*** list the pieces of information
'*** (fields) you will be asking the user
'*** to supply. The only rule is
'*** that each field name should be all
'*** one word, e.g. "MailAddress".
'*** Do not ask for "Email" here (the
'*** form already does that).

        Dim First, Last, MailAddress

'*****************************************

'*****************************************
'*** Now put each piece of information
'*** into the following format:
'*** Field = Request.Form("Field").

        First = Request.Form("First")
        Last = Request.Form("Last")
        MailAddress =
Request.Form("MailAddress")

'*****************************************

Email = Request.Form("Email")

If Email <> "" Then

        If instr(Email, "@") = 0 OR _
        instr(Email, ".") = 0 Then
        Email = "null@noemail.com"
        Else
              Email = Email
        End If
```

```
Else

'****************************************
'*** In case the user leaves their
'*** email address off the form,
'*** this will replace the address so
'*** the email can still be sent.

        Email = "null@noemail.com"
End If

Set Mail = CreateObject("CDONTS.NewMail")
Mail.From = Email

'****************************************
'*** Replace the email address below with
'*** your email address

        Mail.To = "name@domain.com"

'****************************************

Mail.Cc = ""

'****************************************
'*** Replace "Subject goes here" with the
'*** subject line you want each
'*** message to contain, for example:
'*** "Subscription Reservation" or
'*** "Survey Response".

        Mail.Subject = "Subject goes here"

'****************************************

'****************************************
'*** Now replace the text in quotes with
'*** a description of the field,
'*** and replace the text between the &s
'*** with the field names you chose
'*** in the first step above.
```

```
        Body = Body & "First Name: " &_
First & vbCrLf
        Body = Body & "Last Name: " &_
Last & vbCrLf
        Body = Body & " Address: " &_
MailAddress & vbCrLf

'*****************************************

Mail.Body = Body
Mail.Host = "localhost"
Mail.Send
set Mail = nothing

'*****************************************
'*** This is where you direct your form
'*** to a "thank you" page. Just
'*** put the thank you page's name
'*** between the quotes below.

        Response.Redirect("thanks.asp")

'*****************************************

%>

<%
 End Sub
%>

<title>Contact Form</title>
</head>

<body>

<!--
**********************************
*** Put the form's title here -->

        <H3>Name of Form</H3>

<!-- *********************** -->
```

```
<form method="post" name="request"
action="contactform.asp">

<!--
*******************************
*** Change each field name below
*** to match the field names you
*** chose in step one
*************************** -->

                <table border="0">
                <tr>
                <td colspan="2"><p>Enter
your information below:</td>
                </tr>
                <td>First Name: </td>
                <td><input type="text"
name="First" size="35"></td>
                </tr>
                <tr>
                <td>Last Name: </td>
                <td><input type="text"
name="Last" size="35"></td>
                </tr>
                <tr>
                <td>Mailing Address: </td>
                <td><input type="text"
name="MailAddress" size="35"></td>
                </tr>
                <tr>
                <td>Email: </td>
                <td><input type="text"
name="Email" size="35"></td>
                </tr>
                <tr>
                <td align="right"
colspan="2">
                <input type="hidden"
name="Action" value="Submit">
                <input type="Reset">
                <input type="submit"
value="Submit"></td>
                </tr>
                </table>
```

```
</form>
</body>
</html>
```

Search engine optimization

The best place to learn about promoting your website and getting high search engine placement is, by far, SelfPromotion.com. This is a free service, but they do ask for donations. If you use them, please consider sending them a couple of bucks.

SelfPromotion.com
www.selfpromotion.com

Search engines

Selfpromotion.com provides a handy tool that will help you submit your web listing to most of the important search engines. But here's a reiteration of the search engines you should be most concerned about:

Yahoo!
www.yahoo.com
Yahoo! charges a ton of money for a category listing. These are the listings you see when you click on one of Yahoo!'s categories and "drill down" to a sub category. Some people will tell you that you absolutely must be listed in a Yahoo! category, but it's probably going to depend on your budget. If you have $299 a year to spend this way, it's probably worth the money. If not, Yahoo! will eventually list you in its

search results (though not its categories) without any effort on your part.

Overture
www.overture.com.
Overture is a "pay per click" search engine, which means that you bid for high-profile listings and you pay every time a searcher clicks on your link. Despite the cost, it is worth getting an Overture account. It is often very difficult to get a high-profile listing the traditional (free) way, and if you don't use Overture, ad banners, or other Internet advertising alternatives your listing may be so deeply buried in every set of search results that the average user will never see you.

Google
www.google.com.
Google is one of the top search engines, but it can be frustrating trying to get a high profile listing there. For some reason their search engine algorithms just aren't very logical, and you may find your magazine about cats gets ranked several hundred places behind someone's personal home page that mentions the cat they once saw in their back yard. But because Google is such a popular engine, you should be sure you are listed there anyway. Google also has a pay-per-click service, which is almost as valuable as the one offered by Overture.

Other search engines

The rest of these search engines aren't as lucrative as Yahoo!, and you may not be able to get high profile listings in any of them. But it is still important to submit to each one. You can do this with SelfPromotion's multiple listing tool, or you can submit your listings on your own by visiting each site individually. Search engines change their listing rules all the time, so be sure you understand each one before you submit. Some may charge you; others may charge only for an expedited listing. All will take weeks (sometimes even months) to actually list you, so be patient.

Aeiwi www.aeiwi.com	**Open Directory** www.dmoz.com
ExactSeek www.exactseek.com	**What-U-Seek** www.whatuseek.com

Double opt-in email lists

One of the best ways to reach new subscribers is by renting a double opt-in mailing list. Be sure you go to a reputable company. Check their credentials. Make sure that their lists really are "double opt-in" before you sign up, or you could end up doing damage to your company's reputation. Following is a list of some of the most popular email marketing companies:

Advertising.com www.advertising.com	MeMail www.memail.com
PostMasterDirect www.postmasterdirect.com	EmailResults.com market.emailresults.com
HTMail www.htmail.com	Yesmail www.yesmail.com

Mailing list brokers

If you decide to use direct mail, you'll need to know where to go to rent a mailing list. This can be expensive, so be sure you are ready to take this step. Also, research these companies carefully before you commit to anything. Be sure their lists are regularly updated, and try to find out where the names come from. Ask them about targeted lists—you want to make sure you're mailing people who have a specific interest in your magazine's subject matter (i.e., people who collect model airplanes). I haven't tried any of these services, so I can't really give you any information on what they're going to be like, or how successful you might be using them. My only advice is to be cautious.

A.B. Data, Ltd. 8050 N. Port Washington Rd. Milwaukee, WI 53217 (414) 352-4404 www.abdata.com	Direct Media 200 Pemberwick Road Greenwich, CT 06830 (203) 532-1000 www.directmedia.com
Accudata America 4210 Metro Parkway, Suite 300 Fort Myers, FL 33916 (800) 732-3440 www.accudata.com	Mail Marketing Inc. 4075 Gordon Baker Road. Scarborough, ON M1W 2P4 Canada (888) 607 8981 www.mailmarketing.com
Direct Mail Connection 2285 Peachtree Road, Suite 225 Atlanta, GA 30309 (800) 257-5242 www.a1mailinglistexpress.com	Midwest Direct Marketing 2222 West 110th Street Cleveland, OH 44102-3512 (216) 251-2500 www.mw-direct.com

Merchant accounts and third party payment processors

You need one of these, but the one you choose will depend a lot on how much you expect to sell. If you're a small-time, low budget publisher, go with one of the third party payment processors. The three most economical ones (that I know of) are:

PayPal
www.paypal.com
Charges 2.9% + 30¢ per transaction
(more fees may apply if you are selling

internationally or have some other special circumstance. Check PayPal's site for a complete breakdown of fees)

CCNow
www.ccnow.com
Charges 9% + $9.99/month

2Checkout
www.2checkout.com
Charges 5.5% + 45¢ per transaction, plus $49 account set-up fee
Unfortunately, I can no longer recommend these guys. I had so much trouble with them blindly canceling orders (without my permission) and rude technical support that I recently abandoned my account in favor of a traditional merchant account.

If you expect to sell more, or if you just don't like the idea of sending your buyers to another company's website, try one of these services:

PayQuake www.payquake.com	"Pay For Play"	"Select"	"Pro"
Set-up Fee:	$0.00	$99.00	$99.00
Monthly Minimum:	$0.00	$0.00	$0.00
Monthly Gateway Fee:	$0.00	$0.00	$0.00
Monthly Service Charge:	$0.00	$9.95	$19.95
Annual Membership Fee:	$49.00	$49.00	$49.00
Discount Rate (Internet) :	3.79%	2.79%	2.39%
Transaction Fee:	50¢	40¢	30¢

Thompson Merchant Services www.thompsonmerchant.com	
Set-up Fee:	$39.00
Monthly Minimum:	$0.00
Monthly Gateway Fee:	$10.00
Monthly Service Charge:	$7.00
Annual Membership Fee:	$0.00
Discount Rate (Internet):	2.27%
Transaction Fee:	28¢

Professional organizations

The Independent Press Association (IPA) is the number one professional organization for independently published magazines. I highly recommend investing in a membership. First, visit their site and have a look at what they offer.

The Independent Press Association
2729 Mission St. #201
San Francisco, CA, 94110-3131
(877) INDYMAG
www.indypress.org

Where to find writers

Advertise on as many online "freelance market" guides as you can. This will help you attract writers *and* customers, as freelance writers will often buy a copy of your magazine before they send you a story idea. Some of the most popular market listings are:

Absolute Write www.absolutewrite.com	**Writers Write** www.writerswrite.com
FreelanceWriting.com www.freelancewriting.com	**WritersWeekly.com*** www.writersweekly.com

*Warning: WritersWeekly.com is *not* publisher-friendly. Be very careful in your dealings with them.

Writer's Market

All serious publishers should be listed in "Writer's Market" if they plan to accept freelance material. To qualify for a listing, you must be a paying market, and you must already have at least one issue in circulation. Contact them at this address and ask them to send you a publisher's questionnaire:

> **Writer's Market**
> 1507 Dana Avenue
> Cincinnati OH 45207
> (513) 531-2690, ext. 287
> wmsupport@fwpubs.com

Yellow pages websites

You may need to track down the telephone numbers and mailing addresses of potential advertisers and non-traditional distributors. Don't go to the library unless you have to—there are plenty of websites that will give you this information electronically. I've found that Superpages is the best, since it allows you to search by state, though its categories can sometimes be a little hard to follow. Try each of the sites listed below; you may find you prefer a different one.

Dex Online Yellow Pages www.dexonline.com	**Switchboard** www.switchboard.com
SMARTpages.com www.smartpages.com	**yellowpages.com** www.yellowpages.com
Superpages www.superpages.com	**YP.Net** www.yp.net

Copyright and libel

It is amazing how little people generally understand about copyright and libel law. Make sure you are not one of the uninformed before you start any kind of magazine project. Publishers in particular are extremely vulnerable to lawsuits, and in this age of hyper-liability you could easily become the victim of someone who is trying to make a fast buck at your expense.

Don't, for example, use images you found on the Internet unless you are sure those images are in the public domain, or if you've obtained the written permission of the copyright owner. It is not true that everything on the Internet is in the public domain, though you may have heard rumors to that extent. It is also not true that you

can take images and text from any website that has not
included a copyright notice. It is also not true that
making a slight modification to someone else's image
will give you the right to use it.

Likewise, you must be very careful when you publish
information about specific people. If you offend someone
—especially someone who is not a "public figure" (actors
and politicians are examples of public figures)—that
person could take you to court. For example, simply
saying that someone "allegedly" committed a crime does
not protect you from a libel lawsuit. Similarly, because of
privacy laws you cannot use the image of an identifiable
person in advertising materials—even if the image you
are using is in the public domain, even though you may
have the right to use that image in editorial material. It is
important to understand the kinds of things you can and
cannot do and say before you attempt to become a
magazine publisher.

There are several excellent books available that will help
you understand libel and copyright law:

**The Copyright Permission and
Libel Handbook: A Step-by-Step
Guide for Writers, Editors, and
Publishers**
Lloyd J. Jassin and Steve C. Schecter

**Kirsch's Handbook of Publishing
Law: For Authors, Publishers,
Editors and Agents**
Jonathan Kirsch

Copyright Plain and Simple
Cheryl Besenjak

**The Public Domain: How to Find
and Use Copyright-Free Writings,
Music, Art & More**
Stephen Fishman

The IPA also has an excellent (and free) set of links aimed specifically at helping magazine publishers understand media law:

> www.indypress.org/toolbox/lawlinks.ht
> ml

Getting insurance

Insurance for publishers is not inexpensive (expect to pay several thousand dollars annually), but it is very highly recommended, especially if you are going to be dealing with sensitive issues or if you plan to ask "tough questions" to the subjects of your articles. Memberships in certain professional organizations can sometimes qualify you for a discount on this type of insurance (though I don't know of any IPA discounts specifically). However, if you're serious about obtaining this kind of protection, the discount you receive will probably be worth the $100 or so membership fee in one of these small-press professional organizations (which will sometimes also qualify you for group medical insurance and other benefits). The two I know of:

> **The Small Publishers Association
> of North America (SPAN)**
> $95 membership
> www.spannet.org

> **Publishers Marketing Association
> (PMA)**
> $109 membership (for companies with
> 1-9 employees)
> www.pma-online.org

In case you want to contact the insurance agencies directly:

ABA/LIBRIS
1655 Lafayette Street, Suite 200
Denver, CO 80218
(866) 542-7471
www.libris.org

Argo Insurance Brokers
2300 Contra Costa Blvd #375
POB 232017
Pleasant Hill, CA 94523
(925) 682-7001
www.publiability.com

Finding inexpensive or free images

Once you understand copyright law, you may want to
know where you can locate public domain images, or
inexpensive images you can use in your magazine. Often,
the public domain is the best place to go for magazines
that are on a budget. Public domain images are
inexpensive or free (paying a photographer or artist
usually is not). Some companies specialize in providing
publishers with inexpensive images. Corbis
(www.corbis.com) is not one of these, even though most
of what they offer comes directly from the public
domain. Instead, try one of the websites listed below.

Government Websites

As a general rule, photographs that were taken by
government employees (while working on assignment
for the government) are in the public domain. That
doesn't mean every image on a government website is in
the public domain; you need to ask to be sure. Check the
site's copyright section, or email/call the appropriate
person if you need to verify the status of an image.
Following are a couple of government websites where
you might be able to find pictures; check your Yahoo!

listings to find others. You may or may not be able to obtain images for free. Even public domain photos can carry a reproduction fee (usually a nominal $25 or so), especially if there isn't a high-resolution copy available online.

Bureau of Land Management www.blm.gov	**U.S. Department of Agriculture** www.usda.gov
The Library of Congress www.loc.gov	**The U.S. State Department** www.state.gov
NASA www.nasa.gov	

Image Brokers

Other companies specialize in distributing images to publishers, and some will charge according to your circulation (the fewer readers you have, the less you will pay). Some of these types of services:

Impact Digitals www.impactdigitals.com	**NewsCom** www.newscom.com
Independent Media Center indymedia.org	**Reuters** pictures.reuters.com

Museums

Museums are a great source of images, but they tend to be the most expensive of the three types of services listed here. Even though museums may hold material that is technically in the public domain (anything published before 1923), they still own the physical work itself, so they have the right to charge you for any reproductions you might want to obtain from them. Try searching Yahoo! for museums that specialize in artwork related to your magazine's subject. Some museums have image galleries and image purchase capabilities on their websites; for others you will have to inquire directly.

BIPAD

You can obtain your BIPAD number (the number that identifies you to a retailer) from the following company:

BIPAD Inc.
12 Main Street, Suite B
Norwalk, CT 06851
(203) 838-1701
info@nscopy.com
www.bipad.com

A BIPAD application costs $300 (a one time fee), but you'll need it if you want your magazine to be sold on the newsstands. Most distributors won't consider you without one.

After you've obtained the BIPAD number, you'll need to get a barcode from the following company:

**Product Identification and
Processing Systems, Inc.**
436 East 87th Street
New York, NY 10128
Voice (888) 783-7439

Fax (212) 410-7795
www.pips.com
infowsp@pips.com

A barcode will cost you $35 for each issue.

The Library of Congress

Your ISSN and copyright registration can be obtained from these two branches of the Library of Congress (respectively):

Library of Congress
National Serials Data Program
101 Independence Avenue, SE
Washington, D.C. 20540-4160
(202) 707-6452
issn@loc.gov
lcweb.loc.gov/issn

Library of Congress
Copyright Office
101 Independence Avenue, S.E.
Washington, D.C. 20559-6000
www.copyright.gov/register/serial.html

Distributors

Following is a list of distributors that are said to be friendly to independent magazines. I've had the best luck with Desert Moon, Emma Marian, Ubiquity, Disticor, EBSCO, and Bernhard DeBoer. Some of the others have either turned me down or ignored my solicitations. It's always wise to call distributors before you send them a copy of your magazine and a request for distribution services. Make sure they distribute publications like yours. Get them to express an interest first.

Bernhard DeBoer Inc. 113 East Centre St. Nutley, NJ 07110 (973) 667-9300	**Gopher News Company** 9000 10th Ave. No. Minneapolis, MN 55427 (763) 546-5300 www.gophernews.com
Benjamin News 1701 Rankin Missoula, MT 59802 (406) 721-7801	**LMPI** 8155 Larrey Anjou QC H1J 2L5 Canada (514) 355-5674
Desert Moon Periodicals 1226A Calle de Commercio Santa Fe, NM 87507 (800) 547-0182 www.dmoon.com	**News Direct** PO Box 199 Alexandria 1435 NSW Australia +61 2 9353 9911 www.newsdirect.com.au
Disticor Magazine Distribution Services 695 Westney Rd. South, Suite 14 Ajax, Ontario L1S 6M9 Canada 905) 619-6565 www.disticor.com	**Small Changes** P.O. Box 19046 Seattle, WA 98109
EBSCO Publishing 10 Estes Street Ipswich, MA 01938 www.ebsco.com	**Turner Subscription Agency** 1005 West Pines Road Oregon, IL 61061-9681 (800) 852-7404
Emma Marian Ltd. 1574 Gulf Road Point Roberts, WA 98281 (604) 253-9363	**Ubiquity Distributors** 607 Degraw St. Brooklyn, NY 11217 (718) 875-5491

Miscellaneous web pages

You can buy software such as QuarkXpress and PhotoShop from a number of different places around the Internet. For the best deal, it pays to compare prices. Cnet lets you search for the software package you're interested in, and then it tells you where you can get the best deal:

CNet
www.cnet.com

You can also try eBay for just about anything you want to buy for your business, including peripherals, software, Pantone swatches, postage scales, etc. Sometimes you get a good deal, sometimes you don't, but it doesn't hurt to give it a try. Beware, though, sometimes eBay deals really are good to be true. When buying electronics, hardware, etc., you should go for products that come in sealed boxes and include full warranties. If you don't, it is very likely you'll get stuck with something that doesn't work. Most eBay sellers are honest, but not all of them are. Buyer beware.

Also be careful of buying software from eBay. Make sure the item comes with box and books, or you won't be able to license it. Some people even sell pirated copies on eBay, so if the auction doesn't have a picture of the actual product (vs. a marketing photo from the software company's website), or it doesn't specifically say it includes the books and box, you have a good reason to be suspicious.

eBay
www.ebay.com

If you can't find your Pantone swatch on eBay, go directly to Pantone's website:

Pantone
www.pantone.com

Most of the time you will be looking for the "process guide" coated or uncoated swatch, but if in doubt about what exactly you need, be sure to ask your printer.

Stamps.com
www.stamps.com

Questions?

If you have any questions about this book or about your magazine project, please feel free to email the author (babell@palfreymedia.com) at any time for up to 60 days after your purchase date.